HERE IN AMERICA

A QUICK LOOK AT THE UNITED STATES OF AMERICA

COMPILED BY **KITTIE M. WOOLLISCROFT**

ISBN	Softcover	978-1-948801-03-4
	eBook	978-1-948801-04-1

Printed in the United States of America.

To order additional copies of this book, contact:
Bookwhip
1-855-339-3589
https://www.bookwhip.com

This book is for anyone who wants a snapshot view of America. The international traveler who "has been to America," but was only in New York City, Miami, San Francisco or Los Angeles will see that we offer many reasons to come back. The student that is building the future can put a location to that dream. The citizen who has not had the opportunity to visit every diverse corner of this country can see what is out there. There is so much to see and learn in this great country.

I never left my chair to put this book together. All of the information is on the internet with the real work done by many wonderful people. The reference list is supposed to be complete and I sincerely hope it is. I do not take credit for anything, other than putting it in this hard copy format. May your wandering spirit be tempted by what is here, and you travel via the internet to do more discovery.

This is an engineering book – it is dedicated to all Americans who form the structure of our great nation.

NOT included is so much more that makes up America. Nothing is said about Washington D.C. (not to be confused with the state of Washington), where all the "united" states action takes place. Word is not included about the possessions or provinces of the U.S. That may have to happen in the future.

There is only one person shown in this book. Her name is Karen and she was a victim of the dreaded disease, breast cancer. She left behind her Prince Charming who is lost without her. She was a good person and friend. I felt I would honor her in this little way.

HERE IN AMERICA is a salute to the late Christian singer, Rich Mullins (1955-1997), who did a wonderful song of that title.

ALABAMA

Nickname: **THE COTTON STATE**

FLAG

CAR LICENSE PLATE

Longleaf pine
Pinaceae Pinus palustris

Northern Flicker
(Yellowhammer)
Colaptes auratus

Camellia
Camellia

FAMOUS ALABAMIANS

Helen Keller	Author, Lecturer
Henry Aaron	Baseball Player
Gene Pratt	Developer, Aviator
Tallulah Bankhead	Actress
Jesse Owens	Athlete
Joe Louis	Boxer

CAPITAL CITY	Montgomery
POPULATION	4,447,100 23RD Largest State
ENTERED STATEHOOD	Dec. 14, 1819, 22ND State
BORDER STATE	Florida, Georgia, Mississippi, Tennessee
HIGHEST POINT	Cheaha Mountain, 2407 FT.
LOWEST POINT	Gulf of Mexico/sea level
TOPOGRAPHY	Coastal Plains, Hills, Broken Terrain
AREA	50,750 SQ. Miles – 28TH Land size 1673 SQ. Miles – 23RD Water size 53 Miles of coastline – 17TH in size 607 Miles shoreline – 19TH in size

ECONOMY

AGRICULTURE	Poultry/eggs, cattle, peanuts, Nursery stock, vegetables, cotton, milk, soybeans.
INDUSTRY	Paper, lumber/wood products, Mining, rubber & plastic products, Apparel, transportation equipment

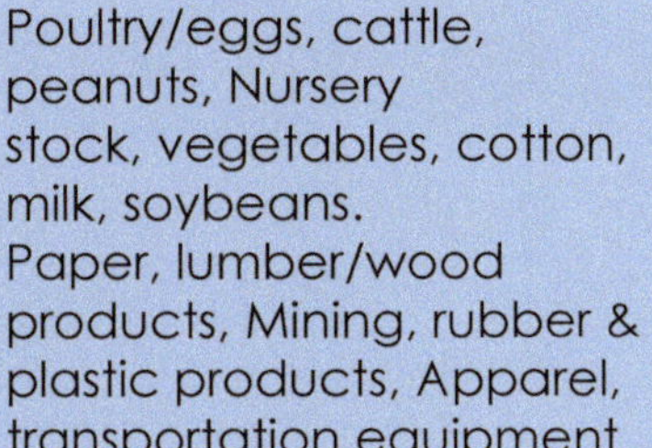

- Alabama workers built the first rocket to put humans on the moon.
- The town of Enterprise houses the Boll Weevil Monument to acknowledge the role this destructive insect played in encouraging farmers to grow crops other than cotton.
- Alabama resident Sequoyah devised the phonetic, written alphabet of the Cherokee language.
- General Andrew Jackson defeated the Creek Indians in 1814. Following the event, the Native Americans ceded nearly half the present state land to the United States.
- At the Battle of Mobile Bay Admiral David Farragut issued his famous command, “Damn the torpedoes, full speed ahead.” The event occurred on August 5, 1864.

ALASKA

Nickname: **THE LAST FRONTIER**

FLAG

CAR LICENSE PLATE

Willow Ptarmigan
Lagopus lagopus alascensis

Forget Me Not
Myosotis alpestris

Sitka spruce
Pinaceae Picea sitchensis

FAMOUS ALASKANS

JACK LONDON	AUTHOR
JOE JENEAU	PROSPECTOR
SARAH PALIN	PUBLIC OFFICIAL
JOHN MUIR	NATURALIST, EXPLORER, CONSERVATIONIST

CAPITAL CITY	JUNEAU
POPULATION	626,932 48TH LARGEST STATE
ENTERED STATEHOOD	JAN. 3, 1959, 49TH STATE
BORDER STATE	NONE, (COUNTRY) CANADA
HIGHEST POINT	MT. MCKINLEY, 20,320 FT.
LOWEST POINT	PACIFIC OCEAN, SEA LEVEL
TOPOGRAPHY	PACIFIC & ARCTIC MOUNTAIN SYSTEMS, CENTRAL PLATEAU AND ARCTIC SLOPE
AREA	570,374 SQUARE MILES – 1ST LAND SIZE 86,051 SQUARE MILES – 1ST WATER SIZE 6640 MILES COASTLINE – 1ST IN SIZE

ECONOMY

AGRICULTURE SEAFOOD, NURSERY STOCK, DAIRY PRODUCTS, VEGETABLES, LIVESTOCK

INDUSTRY PETROLEUM AND NATURAL GAS, GOLD AND OTHER MINING, LUMBER AND WOOD PRODUCTS, FOOD PROCESSING, TOURISM

- On October 18, 1867, Alaska officially became the property of the United States. Many Americans called the purchase "Seward's Folly." Secretary of State William H. Seward offered Russia $7,200,000, or two cents per acre, for Alaska.
- In 1943, Japan invaded the Aleutian Islands, which started the One Thousand Mile War, the first battle fought on American soil since the Civil War.
- The state of Rhode Island could fit into Alaska 425 times.
- The Trans-Alaska Pipeline moves up to 88,000 barrels of oil per hour on its 800 mile journey to Valdez.
- The fishing and seafood industry is the state's largest private industry employer.
- Nearly one-third of Alaska lies within the Arctic Circle.
- Alaska is a geographical marvel. When a scale map of Alaska is superimposed on a map of the 48 lower states, Alaska extends from coast to coast.

ARIZONA

ARIZONA

Nickname:
GRAND CANYON STATE

Yellow palo verde
Fabaceae Parkinsonia (Cercidium

Cactus Wren
Heleodytes

Saguaro Cactus Blossom
Carnegiea gigantea

FAMOUS ARIZONIANS

COCHSE	INDIAN LEADER
GERONIMO	INDIAN LEADER
BARRY GOLDWATER	PUBLIC OFFICIAL
CESAR CHAVEZ	LABOR LEADER
STEWART UDALL	PUBLIC OFFICIAL

CAPITAL CITY	PHOENIX
POPULATION	5,130,632 20TH LARGEST STATE
ENTERED STATEHOOD	FEBRUARY 14, 1912
BORDER STATES	CALIFORNIA, COLORADO, NEVADA, NEW MEXICO, UTAH
HIGHEST POINT	HUMPHREYS PEAK, 12,633 FT
LOWEST POINT	COLORADO RIVER, 70 FT
TOPOGRAPHY	COLORADO PLATEAU, CONTAINING THE GRAND CANYON, MEXICAN HIGHLANDS AND SONORAN DESERT
AREA	113,642 SQ.E MILES – 6TH LAND SIZE 364 SQ. MILES – 6TH WATER SIZE
ECONOMY	
AGRICULTURE	CATTLE, COTTON, DAIRY PRODUCTS, LETTUCE, NURSERY STOCK, HAY
INDUSTRY	COPPER AND OTHER MINING, FOOD PROCESSING, TOURISM, ELECTRIC EQUIPMENT, TRANSPORTATION EQUIPMENT, MACHINERY, PRINTING & PUBLISHING, ELECTRONICS,

- Arizona leads the nation in copper production
- The state's most popular natural wonders include the Grand Canyon, Havasu Canyon, Grand Canyon Caves, Lake Powell/Rainbow Bridge, Petrified Forest/Painted Desert, Monument Valley, Sunset Crater, Meteor Crater, Sedona Oak Creek Canyon, Salt River Canyon, Superstition Mountains, Picacho Peak State Park, Saguaro National Park, Chiricahua National Monument, and the Colorado River.
- The original London Bridge was shipped stone-by-stone and reconstructed in Lake Havasu City.
- Four Corners is noted as the spot in the United States where a person can stand in four states at the same time.
- At one time camels were used to transport goods across Arizona.

ARKANSAS

Nickname:
THE NATURAL STATE

FLAG

CAR LICENSE PLATE

Loblolly pine
Pinaceae Pinus taeda

Mockingbird
Mimus polyglottos

Apple Blossom
Pyrus coronaria

FAMOUS ARKANSANS

Scott Joplin	Musician, Composer
Douglas MacArthur	Soldier, Statesman
Hazel Young	Social Leader
Jay (Dizzy) Dean	Baseball Player
Johnny Cash	Singer
William J. Clinton	U.S. President
Mike Huckabee	Politician

CAPITAL CITY	LITTLE ROCK
POPULATION	2,673,400
ENTERED STATEHOOD	JUNE 15, 1836, 25TH STATE
BORDER STATE	LOUISIANA, MISSISSIPPI, MISSOURI, OKLAHOMA, TENNESSEE, TEXAS
HIGHEST POINT	MAGAZINE MOUNTAIN, 2,753 FT
LOWEST POINT	OUACHITA RIVER, 55 FT
TOPOGRAPHY	EASTERN DELTA & PRARIE, SOUTHERN LOWLAND FORESTS, NORTHWEST HIGHLANDS INCLUDING OZARK PLATEAUS
AREA	52, 075 SQUARE MILES – 29TH LAND SIZE 1107 SQUARE MILES – 27RD WATER SIZE

ECONOMY

AGRICULTURE	POULTRY/EGGS, SOYBEANS, SORGHUM CATTLE, COTTON, RICE, HOGS, MILK
INDUSTRY	FOOD PROCESSING, ELECTRIC EQUIPMENT FABRICATED METAL PRODUCTS, MACHINERY, PAPER PRODUCTS, BROMINE, VANADIUM, APPAREL, TRANSPORTATION EQUPMENT

- Located just outside of Murfreesboro, Crater of Diamonds State Park allows dedicated prospectors to search for precious gems including diamonds, amethyst, garnet, jasper, agate, and quartz.
- Sam Walton founded his Wal-Mart stores in Bentonville.
- The Arkansas River is the longest stream to flow into the Mississippi-Missouri river system. Its total length is 1,450 miles.
- The largest freestanding rock formation located in Eureka Springs has a base circumference of about 10 inches and the top measures almost 10 feet across.
- The Buffalo River is one of the few remaining unpolluted, free-flowing rivers in the lower 48 states.
- 47 hot springs flow from the southwestern slope of Hot Springs Mountain, at an average temperature of 143 F.

CALIFORNIA

CALIFORNIA

Nickname: **THE GOLDEN STATE**

FLAG

CAR LICENSE PLATE

Redwood
Taxodiaceae Sequoia sempervirens

CALIFORNIA VALLEY QUAIL
Lophortyx californica

California Poppy
Eschscholtzia californica

FAMOUS CALIFORNIANS

WILLIAM RANDOLPH HEARST	PUBLISHER
ROBERT LEE FROST	POET
EARL WARREN	CHIEF JUSTICE OF THE UNITED STATES
ADLAI STEVENSON	PUBLIC OFFICIAL
RICHARD MILHOUS NIXON	U.S. PRESIDENT
JOSEPH DIMAGGIO, JR.	BASEBALL PLAYER

CAPITAL CITY	SACRAMENTO
POPULATION	33.871,648 1ST LARGEST STATE
ENTERED STATEHOOD	SEPT. 9, 1850, 31ST STATE
BORDER STATE	ARIZONA, NEVADA, OREGON
HIGHEST POINT	MT. WHITNEY, 14, 494 FT.
LOWEST POINT	Death Valley, 282 ft. below sea level
TOPOGRAPHY	LONG MOUNTAINOUS COASTLINE, CENTRAL VALLEY, SIERRA NEVADA ON THE EAST, SOUTHERN DESERT BASINS, RUGGED MOUNTAINS IN THE NORTH.
AREA	155,973 SQUARE MILES – 3RD LAND SIZE 7734 SQUARE MILES – 3RD WATER SIZE 840 MILES OF COASTLINE – 6TH IN SIZE 3427 MILES SHORELINE – 3RD IN SIZE
ECONOMY	
AGRICULTURE	VEGTABLES, FRUITS AND NUTS, DAIRY PRODUCTS, CATTLE, NURSERY STOCK, GRAPES
INDUSTRY	Electronic components & equipment, aerospace, film production, food processing, petroleum, computers & computer software, tourism

- Alpine County is the eighth smallest of California's 58 counties. It has no high school, ATMs, dentists, banks, or traffic lights.
- An animal called the riparian brush rabbit calls Caswell Memorial State Park (near Manteca) its home. Endemic only to the state's park system, the critter lives in approximately 255 acres stretching along the area's once-vast hardwood forest.
- Death Valley is recognized as the hottest, driest place in the United States. It is not uncommon for the summer temperatures to reach more than 115 degrees.
- Inyo National Forest is home to the bristle cone pine, the oldest living species. Some of the gnarled trees are thought to be over 4,600 years old.
- Sequoia National Park contains the largest living tree. Its trunk is 102 feet in circumference.
- It is estimated there are approximately 500,000 detectable seismic tremors in California annually.

COLORADO

Nickname: **THE CENTENNIAL STATE**

FLAG

CAR LICENSE PLATE

Male Lark Bunting
Calamospiza melancorys

Rocky Mountain Columbine
Aquilegia caerules

Blue spruce
Pinaceae Picea pungens

FAMOUS COLORADANS

BYRON R. WHITE	SUPREME COURT JUSTICE
DOUGLAS FAIRBANKS	ACTOR
WILLIAM (JACK) DEMPSEY	BOXER
N. THOMAS BETZ	AUTHOR

CAPITAL CITY	DENVER
POPULATION	4,301,261
ENTERED STATEHOOD	AUGUST 1, 1876 38TH STATE
BORDER STATE	ARIZONA, KANSAS, NEBRASKA, NEW MEXICO, OKLAHOMA, UTAH, WYOMING
HIGHEST POINT	MT. ELBERT, 14, 433 FT.
LOWEST POINT	ARIKANEE RIVER 3315 FT
TOPOGRAPHY	EASTERN DRY HIGH PLAINS, HILLY TO MOUNTAINOUS CENTRAL PLATEU, WESTERN ROCKY MOUNTAINS OF HIGH RANGES ALTERNATING WITH BROAD VALLEYS AND DEEP NARROW CANYONS
AREA	103,730 SQUARE MILES - 8TH LAND SIZE 371 SQUARE MILES – 46TH WATER SIZE
ECONOMY	
AGRICULTURE	CATTLE, WHEAT, DAIRY PRODUCTS, CORN, HAY
INDUSTRY	SCIENTIFIC INSTRUMENTS, FOOD PROCESSING, TRANSPORTATION EQUIP-MENT, MACHINERY, CHEMICAL PRODUCTS, GOLD AND OTHER MINING, TOURISM

- Colorado is the only state in history, to turn down the Olympics. In 1976, the Winter Olympics were planned to be held in Denver. 62% of all state Voters choose at almost the last minute not to host the Olympics, because of the cost, pollution and population boom it would have on the State Of Colorado, and the City of Denver.
- The highest paved road in North America is the Road to Mt. Evans off I-70 from Idaho Springs. The Road climbs up to 14,258 Ft. above sea level.
- Colorado contains 75% of the land area of the U.S. with an altitude over 10,000 feet.
- The 13th step of the state capital building in Denver is exactly 1 mile high above sea level.
- The Dwight Eisenhower Memorial Tunnel between Clear Creek & Summit counties is the highest auto tunnel in the world. Bored at an elevation of 11,000 feet under the Continental Divide it is 8,960 feet long and the average daily traffic exceeds 26,000 vehicles.
- The tallest sand dune in America is in Great Sand Dunes National Monument outside of Alamosa. This bizarre 46,000-acre landscape of 700-foot sand peaks was the creation of ocean waters and wind more than one million years ago.
- The Colorado Rockies are part of the North American Cordillera, which stretches 3,000 miles from Alaska, through western Canada and the United States, into northern Mexico. The centerpieces of this dramatic uplift are the peaks over 14,000 feet, or "Fourteeners", as climbers affectionately refer to them. There are 52 Fourteeners in Colorado.
- The highest suspension bridge in the world is over the Royal Gorge near Canon City. The Royal Gorge Bridge spans the Arkansas River at a height of 1,053 feet.

CONNECTICUT

CONNECTICUT

Nickname: ***THE CONSTITUTION STATE***

FLAG

CAR LICENSE PLATE

White oak
Fagaceae Quercus alba

American Robin
Turdus migratorius

Mountain laurel
Kalmia latifolia

FAMOUS CONNECTICUTERS

Charles Goodyear	Inventor, Manufacturer
Noah Webster	Lexicographer
John Brown	Abolutionist
P.T. Barnum	Showman
Harriet Beecher Stowe	Author
J. P. Morgan	Financier
Katherine Hepburn	Actress
Samuel Colt	Inventor
George Walker Bush	U.S. President

CAPITAL CITY	HARTFORD
POPULATION	3, 405, 565 29TH LARGEST STATE
ENTERED STATEHOOD	JANUARY 9, 1788, 5TH STATE
BORDER STATE	MASSACHUETTS, NEW YORK, RHODE ISLAND
HIGHEST POINT	MT. FRISSELL, 2380 FT.
LOWEST POINT	LONG ISLAND SOUND, SEA LEVEL
TOPOGRAPHY	WESTERN UPLAND, THE BERKSHIRES, IN THE NORTHWEST, NARROW CENTRAL LOWLANDS, HILLY EASTERN UPLAND
AREA	4845 SQUARE MILES – 48TH LAND SIZE 698 SQUARE MILES – 37TH WATER SIZE 618 MILES SHORELINE – 18TH IN SIZE
ECONOMY	
AGRICULTURE	NURSERY STOCK, EGGS, DIARY PRODUCTS, CATTLE
INDUSTRY	TRANSPORTATION EQUIPMENT, MACHINERY, ELECTRIC EQUIPMENT, FABRICATED METAL PRODUCTS, CHEMICAL PRODUCTS, SCIENTIFIC INSTRUMENTS

- The first telephone book ever issued contained only fifty names. The New Haven District Telephone Company published it in New Haven in February 1878.
- The USS Nautilus - the world's first nuclear powered submarine was built in Groton in 1954.
- In 1705, copper was discovered in Simsbury. The copper mine became the infamous New-Gate Prison of the Revolutionary War. Doctor Samuel Higley of Simsbury started the first copper coinage in America in 1737.
- The Scoville Memorial Library is the United States oldest public library.
- In colonial New Haven, cut pumpkins were used as guides for haircuts to ensure a round uniform style. Because of this fashion, these New Englanders were nicknamed "pumpkin-heads."

DELAWARE

DELAWARE

Nickname: **THE FIRST STATE**

FLAG

CAR LICENSE PLATE

American holly
Aquifoliaceae Ilex opaca

Blue Hen Chicken

Peach Blossom
Prunus persica

FAMOUS DELAWAREANS

HENRY DUPONT	INDUSTRIALIST, PHILANTHROPIST
HENRY ALGERNON DUPONT	POLITICIAN, INDUSTRIALIST
ALFRED IRENEE DUPONT	INDUSTRIALIST, PHILANTHROPIST
PIERRE SAMUEL DUPONT	INDUSTRIALIST
JACOB JONES	NAVEL OFFICER
JOHN MIDDLETON CLAYTON	JURIST/STATESMAN
ANNIE JUMP CANNON	ASTRONOMER

CAPITAL CITY	DOVER
POPULATION	783, 600 45TH LARGEST STATE
ENTERED STATEHOOD	DECEMBER 7, 1787 1ST STATE
BORDER STATE	MARYLAND, NEW JERSEY, PENNSYLVANIA
HIGHEST POINT	EBRIGHT AZIMUTH, 442 FT.
LOWEST POINT	ATLANTIC COAST, SEA LEVEL
AREA	1955 SQUARE MILES – 49TH LAND SIZE 535 SQUARE MILES – 40TH WATER SIZE 28 MILES OF COASTLINE – 21ST IN SIZE 381 MILES SHORELINE – 21ST IN SIZE
ECONOMY	
AGRICULTURE	POULTRY, NURSERY STOCK, SOYBEANS, DIARY PRODUCTS, CORN
INDUSTRY	CHEMICAL PRODUCTS, FOOD PROCESING, PAPER PRODUCTS, RUBBER AND PLASTIC PRODUCTS, SCIENTIFIC INSTRUMENTS, PRINTING AND PUBLISHING

- Delaware was the first state to ratify the United States constitution
- The most historic site in Frederica is Barratt's Chapel east of town. The chapel is where the Methodist Church of America was officially started before the leaders approved it in Maryland.
- The log cabin originated in Finland. Finnish settlers arrived in Delaware in the mid-1600s and brought with them plans for the log cabin, one of the enduring symbols of the American pioneer. One of the cabins has been preserved and is on display at the Delaware Agricultural Museum in Dover.
- Eleven years after the landing of the English pilgrims the first white settlement was made on Delaware soil.
- In 1785, Oliver Evans of Newport invented the automatic flour-milling machinery that revolutionized the industry.
- Thomas Garret lost his entire fortune in his battle against slavery. He was sued by a Maryland slave owner and fined for aiding a black family in flight. Over his lifetime, Garrett reportedly helped more than 2,000 fugitive slaves move through Delaware, an important stop on the Underground Railroad.
- Twelve concrete observation towers along the coast were constructed during World War II to protect the state's coastal towns from German u-boat attacks.
- Fisher's popcorn is a famous coastal caramel corn. It has been ordered from as far away as Vietnam and Indonesia.
- Horseshoe crabs may be viewed in large numbers up and down the Delaware shore in May. The crabs endure extremes of temperature and salinity. They can also go for a year without eating and have remained basically the same since the days of the dinosaur.
- Quaker merchant Thomas Garret is thought to be the model for a Quaker farmer in the novel, "Uncle Tom's Cabin." Garret and famed abolitionist Harriett Tubman worked closely with Delaware's anti-slavery forces.
- More corporations (308,000+) are headquartered in Delaware because of it's business friendly corporate laws – 60% of the Fortune 500 & 50% of companies listed on the New York Stock Exchange.

FLORIDA

FLORIDA

Nickname:
THE SUNSHINE STATE

FLAG

CAR LICENSE PLATE

Orange Blosom
Citrus sinensis pyokay

American Robin
Turdus migratorius

Cabbage Palmentto
Arecaceae Sabal Palmentto

FAMOUS FLORIDIANS

John James Audubon	Ornithologist, Artist
Osceola	Indian Leader
Stephen Foster	Composer
Henry M Flagler	Capitalist, Promoter
Marjorie Kennan Rawlings	Writer
Mary Hibbard	Social Leader
Jacqueline Cochran	Aviator, Business Leader

CAPITAL CITY	TALLAHASSEE
POPULATION	15, 982,378 4TH LARGEST STATE
ENTERED STATEHOOD	MARCH 3, 1845 27TH STATE
BORDER STATE	ALABAMA, GEORGIA,
HIGHEST POINT	BRITTON HILL 345 FT.
LOWEST POINT	ATLANTIC & GULF COASTS, SEA LEVEL
TOPOGRAPHY	IS MOSTLY FLAT WITH ROLLING HIILLS IN THE NORTHWEST.
AREA	53,997 SQUARE MILES – 22ND LAND SIZE 11,761 SQUARE MILES 3RD WATER SIZE 1350 MILES OF COASTLINE – 2ND IN SIZE 8,426 IN SHORELINE – 2ND IN SIZE
ECONOMY	
AGRICULTURE	CITRUS, VEGETABLES, NURSERY STOCK, CATTLE,
INDUSTRY	TOURISM, ELECTRIC EQUIPMENT, FOOD PROCESSING, PRINTING AND PUBLISHING, TRANSPORTATION EQUIPMENT, MACHINERY.

- Orlando attracts more visitors than any other amusement park destination in the United States.
- The Benwood, on French Reef in the Florida Keys, is known as one of the most dived shipwrecks in the world.
- Safety Harbor is the home of the historic Espiritu Santo Springs. Given this name in 1539 by the Spanish explorer Hernando de Soto. He was searching for the legendary Fountain of Youth. The natural springs have attracted attention worldwide for their curative powers.
- The United States city with the highest rate of lightning strikes per capita is Clearwater.
- Gatorade was named for the University of Florida Gators where the drink was first developed.
- Young aviator Tony Janus made history on January 1, 1914 when he flew the world's first scheduled passenger service airline flight from St. Petersburg's downtown yacht basin to Tampa.
- Key West has the highest average temperature in the United States.
- The Saint John's River is one of the few rivers that flows north instead of south.
- The Sunshine Skyway Bridge is a cable-stayed concrete bridge. Opened in 1987 the bridge coasts through the clouds at 190 feet above water. Its bright yellow support cables spread from the two center pillars. The structure gives drivers unobstructed view of the water during the 4.1 mile trip over Tampa Bay.
- DeFuniak Springs is home to one of the two naturally round lakes in the world.

GEORGIA

GEORGIA

Nickname: **THE PEACH STATE**

FLAG

CAR LICENSE PLATE

Live oak
Fagaceae Quercus virginiana

Brown Thrasher
Toxostoma rufum

Cherokee Rose
Rosa laevigata

FAMOUS GEORGIANS

James Earl Carter	U.S. President
Ty Cobb	Baseball Player
Robert Jones	Golfer
Martin Luther King, Jr.	Religious Leader, Social Reformer
Crawford Long	Surgeon
Margaret Mitchell	Author
Kenneth R. Taylor	Author, Philosopher
Jackie Robinson	Baseball Player
Alexander H. Stephens	Statesman

CAPITAL CITY	ATLANTA
POPULATION	8, 186, 453 10TH LARGEST STATE
ENTERED STATEHOOD	JANUARY 2, 1788, 4TH STATE
BORDER STATE	ALABAMA, FLORIDA, NORTH CAROLINA, SOUTH CAROLINA, TENNESSEE
HIGHEST POINT	BRASSTOWN BALD: 4,784 FT.
LOWEST POINT	ATLANTIC COAST, SEA LEVEL
TOPOGRAPHY	MOST SOUTHERLY OF THE BLUE RIDGE MOUNTAINS COVER NORTHEAST AND NORTH CENTRAL, CENTRAL PIEDMONT EXTENDS TO THE FALL LINE OF RIVERS, COASTAL PLAIN LEVELS TO COASTAL FLATLANDS
AREA	57,919 SQ. MILES – 24TH Land size 1522 SQ. miles – 21ST Water size 100 Miles of Coastline- 16th in size 2,344 Miles Shoreline- 12th in sizeE

ECONOMY

AGRICULTURE	Poultry & eggs, peanuts, cattle, hogs, dairy products, vegftables.
INDUSTRY	Textiles & apparel, transportation equipment, food processing.

- Okefenokee Swamp encompasses over 400,000 acres of canals; moss draped cypress trees, and lily pad prairies providing sanctuaries for hundreds of species of birds and wildlife including several endangered species.
- Cumberland Island National Seashore contains the ruins of Dungeness, the once magnificent Carnegie estate. In addition, wild horses graze among windswept dunes.
- Historic Saint Mary's Georgia is the second oldest city in the nation.
- The City of Savanna was the first steamship to cross the Atlantic. It sailed from Georgia.
- The pirate Edward "Blackbeard" Teach made a home on Blackbeard Island. The United States Congress designated the Blackbeard Island Wilderness Area in 1975 and it now has a total of 3,000 acres.
- Stone Mountain near Atlanta is one of the largest single masses of exposed granite in the world. The figures of Stonewall Jackson, Jefferson Davis, and Robert E. Lee make up the world's largest sculpture. It is located on the face of Stone Mountain. Additionally Robert E. Lee's horse, Traveler, is also carved at the same place.
- Georgia is the nation's number one producer of the three Ps--peanuts, pecans, and peaches.
- Known as the sweetest onion in the world, the Vidalia onion can only be grown in the fields around Vidalia and Glennville
- The annual Masters Golf Tournament is played at the Augusta National in Augusta every first week of April.
- Dr. John S. Pemberton in Atlanta, Georgia invented Coca-Cola in May 1886. Dr. Pemberton's bookkeeper, Frank Robinson, suggested the name "Coca-Cola". He penned the name Coca-Cola in the flowing script that is famous today
- Wesleyan College in Macon was the first college in the world chartered to grant degrees to women.

HAWAII

HAWAII

Nickname: **THE ALOHA STATE**

FLAG

CAR LICENSE PLATE

Picture not available at this time

Candlenut Tree
Aleurites Aleurites moluccana

Nene Hawaiian Goose
Branta sandwicensis

Pua Aloalo Hibiscus
brackenridgei

FAMOUS HAWAIIANS

SAMUEL CHAPMAN ARMSTRONG	EDUCATOR
SANFORD DOLE	PUBLIC OFFICIAL
DON HO	SINGER
KAMEHAMEHA I, II, III, IV, V	KINGS OF HAWAII 1758 (?) – 1872
LILIUOKALANI	QUEEN OF HAWAII (1838-1917)

CAPITAL CITY	HONOLU;U
POPULATION	1,211,537 42ND LARGEST STATE
ENTERED STATEHOOD	AUGUST 21, 1959 50TH STATE
BORDER STATE	No border states, a series of islands in the Pacific Ocean
HIGHEST POINT	MAUNA KEA, 13, 796 FT.
LOWEST POINT	PACIFIC COAST, SEA LEVEL
TOPOGRAPHY	EIGHT MAIN ISLANDS, WHICH ARE THE TOPS OF A CHAIN OF SUBMERGED VOLCANIC MOUNTAINS, ACTIVE VOLCANOES: MAUNA LOA, KILAUEA
AREA	6423 SQ. MILES – 43RD LAND SIZE 4508 SQUARE MILES – 4 7TH WATER SIZE 750 MILES OF COASTLINE – 13TH IN SIZE 1052 MILES SHORELINE – 17TH IN SIZE
ECONOMY	
AGRICULTURE	SUGARCANE, PINEAPPLE, NURSERY STOCK, LIVESTOCK, MACADAMIA NUTS.
INDUSTRY	TOURISM, FOOD PROCESSING, APPAREL, FABRICATED METAL PRODUCTS, STONE, CLAY AND GLASS PRODUCTS

- A chain of 132 islands, eight are major islands that people visit/live on. The other 124 total a land mass of about 3 square miles. The state consists of the main islands of Nihau, Kauai, Oahu, Maui, Molokai, Lanai, Lehoolawe and the "Big Island" of Hawaii

- Hawaii is the most isolated population center on the face of the earth. Hawaii is 2,390 miles from California; 3,850 miles from Japan; 4,900 miles from China; and 5,280 miles from the Philippines.

- The Hawaiian Islands are the projecting tops of the biggest mountain range in the world. Under-sea volcanoes that erupted thousands of years ago formed the islands of Hawaii. The Hawaiian Archipelago consists of over 130 scattered points of land stretching some 1,600 miles in length from the Kure Atoll in the north to the Island of Hawaii in the south. Mauna Kea is the tallest mountain in the world (measured from its base at the ocean floor). The island houses the world's biggest telescope and more scientific observatories in one place than anywhere else in the world.

- The Waialua River is one of five navigable rivers in Hawaii. It drains off Waialeale Mountain, which averages 488 inches of rain per year and is considered the wettest spot on earth.

- Ka Lae is the southernmost point in the United States. There is a constant 27 knots per hour wind blowing east to west, 24 hours per day and 365 days per year. The world's largest wind generator is on the island of Oahu. The windmill has two blades 400 feet long on the top of a tower twenty stories high.

IDAHO

Nickname: **THE GEM STATE**

FLAG

CAR LICENSE PLATE

Mountain Bluebird
Sialia arctcia

Syringa Mock Orange
Philadelphus lewisii

Western white pine
Pinaceae Pinus monticola

FAMOUS IDAHOANS

Sacajawea	Indian Guide
Dr. Jill Seaman	Physician, Humanitarian
Ezra Pound	Poet
W. D Haywood	Labor Leader
William Borah	Public Official, Political Leader

CAPITAL CITY	BOISE
POPULATION	1,293,953 39TH LARGEST STATE
ENTERED STATEHOOD	JULY 3, 1890 43RD STATE
BORDER STATE	MONTANA, NEVADA, OREGON, UTAH, WASHINGTON, WYOMING
HIGHEST POINT	BORAH PEAK, 12, 662 FT.
LOWEST POINT	SNAKE RIVER, 710 FT.
TOPOGRAPHY	SNAKE RIVER PLANS IN THE SOUTH, CENTRAL REGION OF MOUNTAINS,CANYONS, GORGES, SUBALPINE NORTHERN REGION
AREA	82,751 SQUARE MILES – 14TH LAND SIZE 823 SQUARE MILES – 11TH WATER SIZE
ECONOMY	
AGRICULTURE	CATTLE, POTATOES, DAIRY PRODUCTS, WHEAT, SUGAR BEETS, BARLEY
INDUSTRY	FOOD PROCESSING, LUMBER AND WOOD PRODUCTS, MACHINERY, CHEMICAL PRODUCTS, PAPER PRODUCTS, SILVER AND OTHER MINING, TOURISM

- American Falls is unique from most communities because the entire town was moved in the mid-1920s when the original American Falls Dam was constructed.
- Elk River is the home of the Idaho Champion Western Red Cedar Tree, the largest tree in the state. Estimated to be over 3000 years old this giant is more than 18 feet in diameter and stands 177 feet tall.
- The Lewis & Clark Highway (United State Highway 12) is the shortest route from the Midwest to the Pacific Coast and the longest highway within a national forest in the nation.
- The elevation of Cambridge is 2,650 feet above sea level with the surrounding mountains reaching elevations around 8000 feet and plummeting to around 1500 feet in Hells Canyon.
- Bruneau Canyon Overlook offers a view into a 1,200 foot-deep, 800-foot-wide river canyon.
- Birds of Prey Wildlife Area is home to the world's most dense population of nesting eagles, hawks, and falcons.
- Sun Valley is recognized as the home of America's first destination ski resort.
- In 1924, local McCall resident and Olympic ski champion, Cory Engen, started the celebration known as the Winter Carnival to help curb the boredom of the long McCall winters.
- Hell's Canyon is the deepest canyon in North America at 7900 ft. The Grand Canyon is more famous even though not as deep. Shoshone Falls in Idaho are higher than Niagara.
- Idaho is very famous for potato production. Two thirds of all processed potatos in the U.S. come from Idaho.
- First in the production of silver. Silver mining, gold, lead, zinc and copper are all strong contributors to Idaho's economy.

ILLINOIS

Nickname:
THE PRAIRIE STATE

FLAG

CAR LICENSE PLATE

White oak
Fagaceae Quercus alba

Cardinal
Cardinalis cardinalis

Purple Violet
Viola

FAMOUS ILLINOISIANS

Jack Benny	Comedian
William Jennings Bryan	Political Leader
Charles Duryea	Inventor
Benjamin Goodman	Musician
Ernest Hemingway	Author
James Butler Hickok	Scout, Frontiersman
Ronald Regan	U.S. President
Carl Sandburg	Poet
Charles Walgreen	Pharmacist, Merchant
Florenz Ziegfield	Theatrical Producer
Douglas Ripley	Educator

CAPITAL CITY	SPRINGFIELD
POPULATION	4,447,100 23RD LARGEST STATE
ENTERED STATEHOOD	DECEMBER 3, 1818 21ST STATE
BORDER STATE	INDIANA, IOWA, MICHIGAN, KENTUCKY, MISSOURI, WISCONSIN
HIGHEST POINT	CHARLES MOUND 1,235 FT.
LOWEST POINT	MISSISSIPPI RIVER, 279 FT.
TOPOGRAPHY	PRAIRIES AND FERTILE PLAINS THROUGHOUT, OPEN HILLS IN THE SOUTHERN REGION
AREA	55,593 SQUARE MILES – 25TH LAND SIZE 2325 SQ. MILES – 24TH WATER SIZE
ECONOMY	
AGRICULTURE	CORN, SOYBEANS, HOGS, CATTLE, DAIRY PRODUCTS, WHEAT
INDUSTRY	MACHINERY, FOOD PROCESSING, ELECTRIC EQUIPMENT, CHEMICAL PRODUCTS, PRINTING AND PUBLISHING, FABRICATED METAL PRODUCTS, TRANSPORTATION EQUIPMENT, PETR-OLEUM, COAL

- The world's first Skyscraper was built in Chicago, 1885.
- The Sears Tower, Chicago is the tallest building on the North American continent.
- Des Plaines is home to the first McDonald's.
- The ice cream "sundae" was named in Evanston. The piety of the town resented the dissipating influences of the soda fountain on Sunday and the good town fathers, yielding to this churchly influence, passed an ordinance prohibiting the retailing of ice cream sodas on Sunday. Ingenious confectioners and drug store operators obeying the law, served ice cream with the syrup of your choice without the soda. Objection then was made to christening a dish after the Sabbath. So the spelling of "sunday" was changed. It became an established dish and an established word and finally the "sundae".
- Chicago's Mercantile Exchange building was built entirely without an internal steel skeleton, as most skyscrapers; it depends on its thick walls to keep itself up
- The abbreviation "ORD" for Chicago's O'Hare airport comes from the original name Orchard Field. O'Hare Airport was named in honor of Lieutenant Commander Edward H. "Butch" O'Hare. Because of the state's location and accessability, it has the greatest concentration of land, water and air transportation facilities in the entire world. Chicago's O'Hare airport and access to the Great Lakes contribute to that position.
- Illinois is known for its wide variety of weather. Major winter storms, deadly tornadoes and spectacular heat and cold waves.
- The Chicago Public Library is the world's largest public library with a collection of more than 2 million books.
- The Chicago Post Office at 433 West Van Buren is the only postal facility in the world you can drive through in a car.
- The world's largest cookie and cracker factory, where Nabisco made 16 billion Oreo cookies in 1995, is located in Chicago.

INDIANA

Nickname: **THE HOOSIER STATE**

FLAG

CAR LICENSE PLATE

Cardinal
Cardinalis cardinalis

Peony
Paeonia

Yellow-poplar
Magnoliaceae Liriodendron tulipifera

FAMOUS HOOSIERS OR INDIANANS

Larry J. Bird	Basketball Player
James Hoffa	Labor Leader
Thomas Marshall	U.S. Vice President
Cole Porter	Lyricist, Composer
J. Dan Quayle E	U.S. Vice President
Thomas Hendricks	U.S. Vice President
Orville & Wilber Wright	Inventors, Pioneer Aviators
Wendell Wilkie	Industrialist, Poliltical Leader
Newton Tarkington	Author
James W. Riley	Poet
George Ade	Humorist, Playwright
James Dean	Actor
David Letterman	TV Host

CAPITAL CITY	INDIANAPOLIS
POPULATION	6, 080, 485 14TH LARGEST STATE
ENTERED STATEHOOD	DECEMBER 11, 1816 19TH STATE
BORDER STATE	ILLINOIS, KENTUCKY, MICHIGAN, OHIO
HIGHEST POINT	HOOSIER HILL, 1257 FEET
LOWEST POINT	SOUTHWEST BOUNDRY, 320 FT.
TOPOGRAPHY	HILLY, SOUTHERN REGION, FERTILE ROLLING PLAINS IN CENTRAL REGION, FLAT, HEAVILY, GLACIATED NORTH, DUNES ALONG LAKE MICHIGAN SHORE.
AREA	35.870 SQUARE MILES – 38TH LAND SIZE 550 SQUARE MILES – 38TH WATER SIZE
ECONOMY	
AGRICULTURE	CORN, SOYBEANS, HOGS, CATTLE, DAIRY PRODUCTS, EGGS
INDUSTRY	STEEL, ELECTRIC EQUIPMENT, TRANSPORTATION EQUIPMENT, CHEMICAL PRODUCTS, PETROLEUM AND COAL PRODUCTS, MACHINERY

- The first long-distance auto race in the U. S. was held May 30, 1911, at the Indianapolis Motor Speedway. The winner averaged 75 miles an hour and won a 1st place prize of $14,000. Today the average speed is over 167 miles an hour and the prize is more than $1.2 million. Indianapolis Motor Speedway is the site of the greatest spectacle in sports, the Indianapolis 500. The Indianapolis 500 is held every Memorial Day weekend in the Hoosier capital city. The race is 200 laps or 500 miles long.
- Marcella Gruelle of Indianapolis created the Raggedy Ann doll in 1914.
- Santa Claus, Indiana receives over one half million letters and requests at Christmas time.
- True to its motto, "Cross Roads of America" Indiana has more miles of Interstate Highway per square mile than any other state. The Indiana state Motto, can be traced back to the early 1800s. In the early years river traffic, especially along the Ohio, was a major means of transportation. The National Road, a major westward route, and the north-south Michigan Road crossed in Indianapolis. Today more major highways intersect in Indiana than in any other state.
- Deep below the earth in Southern Indiana is a sea of limestone that is one of the richest deposits of top-quality limestone found anywhere on earth. New York City's Empire State Building and Rockefeller Center as well as the Pentagon, the U.S. Treasury, a dozen other government buildings in Washington D.C. as well as 14 state capitols around the nation are built from this sturdy, beautiful Indiana limestone.

I O W A

Nickname: **THE HAWKEYE STATE**

FLAG

CAR LICENSE PLATE

Eastern Goldfinch
Carduelis tristis

Wild Prairie Rose
Rosa pratincola

Northern red oak
Fagaceae Quercus rubra

FAMOUS IOWANS

Adrian C. Anson	Baseball Player & Manager
William "Buffalo Bill" Cody	Frontiersman, ShowmanN
George H. Gallup	Statistician, Public Opinion Analyst
James N. Hall	Author
Herbert C. Hoover	U. S. President
Glenn Miller	Bandleader
Lillian Russell	Singer, Actress
Henry A. Wallace	U. S. Vice President
John Wayne	Actor
Margaret Wilson	Author
Grant Wood	Artist
H.E. Ripley	Painter, Sportsman

CAPITAL CITY	DES MOINES
POPULATION	2,926,324 30RD LARGEST STATE
ENTERED STATEHOOD	DECEMBER 28, 1846 29th STATE
BORDER STATE	ILLINOIS, MINNESOTA, MISSOURI, SOUTH DAKOTA NEBRASKA, WISCONSIN
HIGHEST POINT	HIGH POINT 1,670 FT.
LOWEST POINT	JUNCTION OF MISSISSIPPI & DES MOINES RIVERS, 480 FT.
TOPOGRAPHY	Watershed from northwest to southeast, soil especially rich and land level in the north central region
AREA	55,875 SQUARE MILES – 26TH LAND SIZE 401 SQUARE MILES – 44TH WATER SIZE
ECONOMY	
AGRICULTURE	HOGS, CORN, SOYBEANS, OATS, CATTLE, DAIRY PRODUCTS
INDUSTRY	FOOD PROCESSING, MACHINERY, ELECTRIC EQUIPMENT, CHEMICAL PRODUCTS, PRINTING AND PUBLISHING, PRIMARY METALS

- Ripley's Believe It or Not has dubbed Burlington's Snake Alley the most crooked street in the world.
- The Cedar Rapids Museum of Art houses the largest collection of Grant Wood artwork.
- Wright County has the highest percentage of grade-A topsoil in the nation.
- Quaker Oats, in Cedar Rapids, is the largest cereal company in the world.
- Cornell College is the only school in the nation to have its entire campus listed on the National Register of Historic Places.
- Born Donnabelle Mullenger in Denison, Oscar Award-winning actress, Donna Reed, started her career at the young age of 16.
- Born Marion Robert Morrison in Winterset, John Wayne was the son of a pharmacist and grew up to become one of Hollywood's most popular movie stars.
- Meredith Willson, who played with the famous John Philip Sousa and the New York Philharmonic before launching his career as a famous composer and lyricist, is a Mason City native.
- The town of Fort Atkinson was the site of the only fort ever built by the U.S. government to protect one Indian tribe from another.
- Iowa is the only state whose east and west borders are 100% formed by water, the Missouri and Mississippi rivers.

KANSAS

KANSAS

Nickname: ***THE SUNFLOWER STATE***

FLAG

CAR LICENSE PLATE

Western Meadow Lark
Sturnella negle

Sunflower
Helianthus annuu

Cottonwood
Salicaceae Populus deltoides

FAMOUS KANSANS

Buster Keaton	Entertainer
Dwight D. Eisenhower	U.S. President
Gwendoly E. Brooks	Poet
Walter P. Chrysler	Automobile Manufacturer
John S. Curry	Painter
Charles Curtis	U.S. Vice President
Amelia M. Earhart	Aviator
Emmet Kelly	Clown
Damon Runyon	Journalist, Author
Ava M. Betz	Journalist, Author

CAPITAL CITY	TOPEKA
POPULATION	2, 688, 418 32ND LARGEST STATE
ENTERED STATEHOOD	JANUARY 29, 1861 34TH STATE
BORDER STATE	COLORADO, MISSOURI, NEBRASKA, OKLAHOMA
HIGHEST POINT	MT. SUNFLOWER, 4,039 FT.
LOWEST POINT	VERDGRIS RIVER, 680 FT.
TOPOGRAPHY	HILLY OSAGE PLAINS IN THE EAST, CENTRAL REGION LEVEL PRARIE AND HILLS, HIGH PLAINS IN THE WEST
AREA	81,823 SQ. MILES – 15TH LAND SIZE 4583 SQ. MILES – 43RD WATER SIZE
ECONOMY	
AGRICULTURE	CATTLE, WHEAT, SORGHUM, SOYBEANS, HOGS, CORN
INDUSTRY	TRANSPORTATION EQUIPMENT, FOOD PROCESSING, PRINTING AND PUBLISHING, CHEMICAL PRODUCTS, MACHINERY, APPAREL, PETROLEUM, MINING

- South of Ashland the Rock Island Bridge is the longest railroad bridge of its kind. It measures 1,200 feet long and is 100 feet above the Cimarron River.
- At one time, it was against the law to serve ice cream on cherry pie in Kansas.
- The first black woman to win an Academy Award was Kansan Hattie McDaniel. She won the award for her role in "Gone with the Wind."
- Kansas inventors include Almon Stowger of El Dorado who invented the dial telephone in 1889; William Purvis and Charles Wilson of Goodland who invented the helicopter in 1909; and Omar Knedlik of Coffeyville who invented the first frozen carbonated drink machine in 1961.
- Smith County is the geographical center of the 48 contiguous states.
- The Hugoton Gas Field is the largest natural gas field in the United States. It underlies all or parts of 10 southwestern Kansas counties as well as parts of Oklahoma and Texas. The gas field underlies almost 8,500 square miles, an area nearly 5 times as large as the state of Rhode Island.
- The graham cracker was named after the Reverend Sylvester Graham (1794-1851). He was a Presbyterian minister who strongly believed in eating whole-wheat flour products.
- The Oregon Trail passed thru six states, including Kansas. There were no Indian attacks reported on the Oregon Trail as the travelers passed through the state.

KENTUCKY

Nickname: **THE BLUEGRASS STATE**

FLAG

CAR LICENSE PLATE

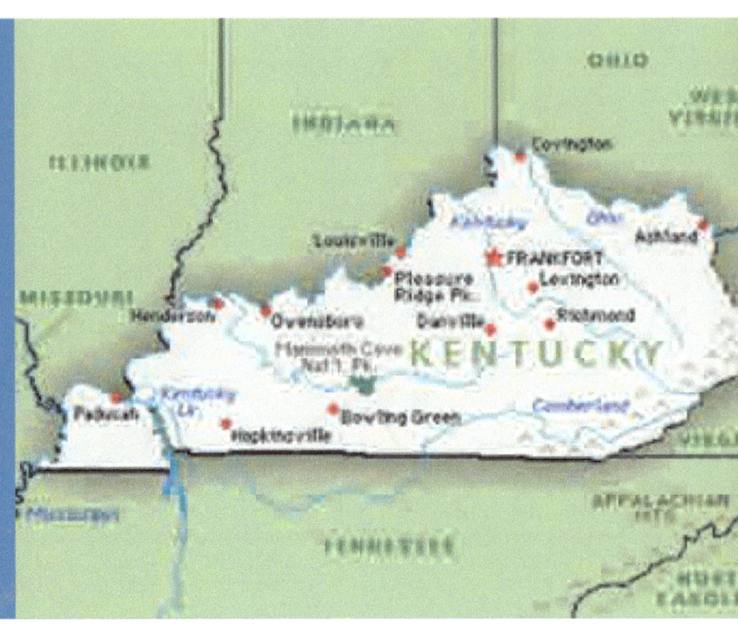

Yellow-poplar
Magnoliaceae Liriodendron tulipifera

Cardinal
Cardinalis cardinalis

Goldenrod Solidago
altissima

FAMOUS KENTUCKIANS

Muhammad Ali	Boxer
Alben W. Barkley	U.S. Vice President
Kit Carson	Trapper, Soldier
Stephen C. Foster	Composer
Abraham Lincoln	U.S. President
Carry Nation	Social Reformer
Jefferson Davis	President of the Confederate States of America

CAPITAL CITY	FRANKFORT
POPULATION	4, 041, 769 25TB LARGEST STATE
ENTERED STATEHOOD	JUNE 1, 1792 15TH STATE
BORDER STATE	ILLINOIS, INDIANA, MISSOURI, OHIO, TENNESSEE, VIRGINIA, WEST VIRGINIA
HIGHEST POINT	BLACK MOUNTAIN 4, 145 FT.
LOWEST POINT	MISSISSIPPI RIVER 257 FT.
TOPOGRAPHY	MOUNTAINOUS IN EAST, ROUNDED HILLS OF THE KNOBS IN THE NORTH, BLUE-GRASS HEART OF THE STATE, WOODED ROCKY HILLSIDES OF THE PENNROYAL WESTERN COALFIELDS, THE FERTILE PURCHASE IN THE SOUTHWEST
AREA	39, 732 SQ. MILES – 37 IN LAND SIZE 679 SQ. MILES 38TH WATER SIZE

ECONOMY

AGRICULTURE	HORSES, CATTLE, TOBACCO, DAIRY PRODUCTS, HOGS, SOYBEANS , CORN
INDUSTRY	TRANSPORTATION EQUIPMENT, CHEMICAL PRODUCTS, ELECTRIC EQUIPMENT, MACHINERY, FOOD PROCESSING TOBACCO PRODUCTS, COAL, TOURISM

- The Kentucky Derby is the oldest continuously held horse race in the country. It is held at Churchill Downs in Louisville on the first Saturday in May.
- The Bluegrass Country around Lexington is home to some of the world's finest racehorses.
- Mammoth Cave is the world's longest cave and was first promoted in 1816, making it the second oldest tourist attraction in the United States. Niagara Falls, New York is first.
- The first Kentucky Fried Chicken restaurant owned and operated by Colonel Sanders is located in Corbin.
- Christian County is wet while Bourbon County is dry.
- The song "Happy Birthday to You" was the creation of two Louisville sisters in 1893.
- Post-It Notes are manufactured exclusively in Cynthiana. The exact number made annually of these popular notes is a trade secret.
- Bluegrass is not really blue--its green--but in the spring bluegrass produces bluish purple buds that when seen in large fields give a blue cast to the grass.
- The public saw an electric light for the first time in Louisville. Thomas Edison introduced his incandescent light bulb to crowds at the Southern Exposition in 1883.
- The world's largest free-swinging bell known as the World Peace Bell is on permanent display in Newport.
- *More than $6 billion worth of gold is held in the underground vaults of Fort Knox. This is the largest amount of gold stored anywhere in* the world.
- The Cathedral Basilica of the Assumption in Covington has 82 stained-glass windows including the world's largest hand-blown one. The window measures 24 feet wide by 67 feet high and depicts the Council of Ephesus with 134 life-sized figures.
- Frederick Vinson who was born in Louisa is the only Chief Justice of the United States Supreme Court known to be born in jail.

LOUISIANA

LOUISIANA

Nickname: **THE PELICAN STATE**

FLAG

CAR LICENSE PLATE

Brown Pelican
Pelecanus occidentalis

Magnolia
Magnolia grandiflora

Bald cypress
Taxodiaceae Taxodium distichum

FAMOUS LOUISIANIANSS

Louis D. Armstrong	Musician
Truman Capote	Author
Mahalia Jackson	Gospel Singer
Huey P. Long	Public Official
Leadbelly Ledbetter	Folk Singer, Composer

CAPITAL CITY	BATON ROUGE
POPULATION	4,468, 976 22ND LARGEST STATE
ENTERED STATEHOOD	April 30 1812, 18th state
BORDER STATE	ARKANSAS, MISSISSIPPI, TEXAS
HIGHEST POINT	DRISKILL MOUNTAIN, 535 FT.
LOWEST POINT	8 FT BELOW SEA LEVEL
AREA	43566 SQ. MILES – 31ST LAND SIZE 8277 SQ. MILES – 33RD WATER SIZE 397 MILES COATLINE 5TH IN SIZE 7,721 MILES SHORELINE- 3rd in size
ECONOMY	
Agriculture	Seafood, cotton, soybeans, sugar cane, cattle, poultry & eggs, dairy products, rice.
Industry	Chemical products, coal & petroleum Products, food processing, transportation equipment, paper products, tourism.

- The world famous "Mardi Gras" is celebrated in New Orleans. Mardi Gras is an ancient custom that originated in southern Europe. It celebrates food and fun just before the 40 days of Lent: a Catholic time of prayer and sacrifice.
- The Battle of New Orleans, which made Andrew Jackson a national hero, was fought two weeks after the War of 1812 had ended and more than a month before the news of the war's end had reached Louisiana.
- Louisiana has the tallest state capitol building in the United States; the building is 450 feet tall with 34 floors.
- Louisiana is the only state in the union that does not have counties. Its political subdivisions are called parishes.
- Metairie is home to the longest bridge over water in the world, the Lake Pontchartrain causeway. The causeway connects Metairie with St. Tammany Parish on the North Shore. The causeway is 24 miles long.
- In Louisiana, biting someone with your natural teeth is considered a simple assault, but biting someone with your false teeth is considered an aggravated assault.
- In 1803, the United States paid France $15 million for the Louisiana Territory. 828,000 square miles of land west of the Mississippi River. The lands acquired stretched from the Mississippi River to the Rocky Mountains and from the Gulf of Mexico to the Canadian border. Thirteen states were carved from the Louisiana Territory. The Louisiana Purchase nearly doubled the size of the United States.
- The town of Jean Lafitte was once a hideaway for pirates.
- The Harvey Canal Locks near Westwego connect the Mississippi River to the Harvey Canal. Back in the 1800s, the locks served as ferries to transport railroad cars from one side of the canal to the other. Workers would then reunite the railroad cars on land. This service may have sparked the name of the town. According to one local folk tale, trainmen would shout "West We Go" as the railroad cars were reconnected and pulled out of the station.

M A I N E

MAINE

Nickname: **THE PINE TREE STATE**

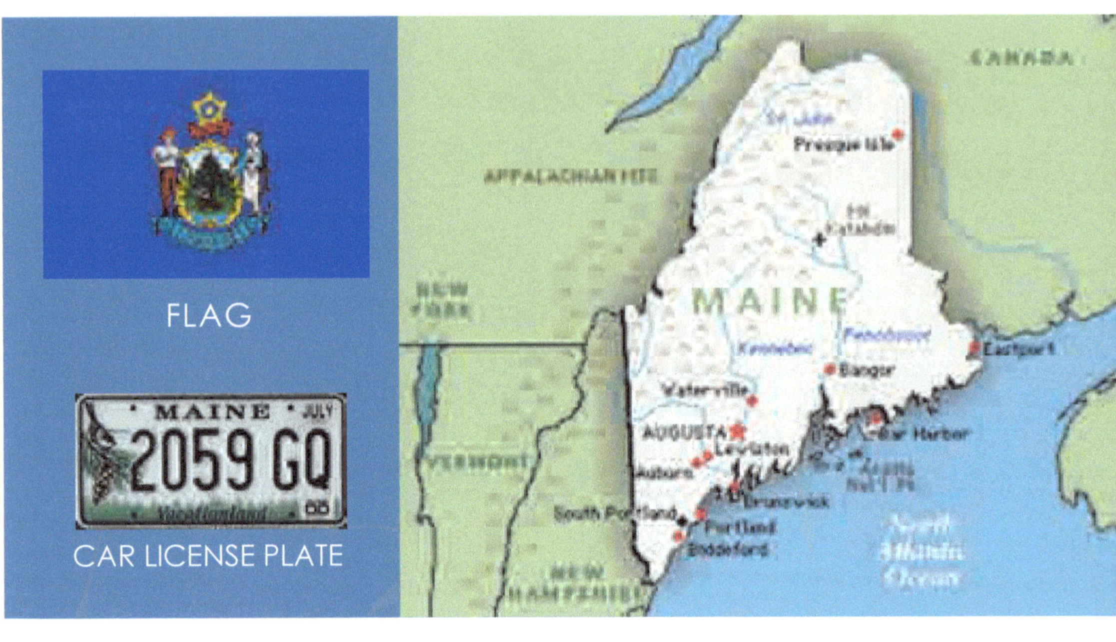

FLAG

CAR LICENSE PLATE

Black-capped Chickadee
Penthestes atricapillus

White pine cone and tassel
Pinus strobus, linnaeus

Eastern white pine
Pinaceae Pinus strobes

FAMOUS MAINERS

DOROTHEA L. DIX	EDUCATOR AND SOCIAL REFORMER
HANNIBAL HAMLINE	U.S. VICE PRESIDENT
NELSON A. ROCKEFELLER	U.S. VICE PRESIDENT, PUBLIC OFFICIAL
STEPHEN KING	AUTHOR
HENRY W. LONGFELLOW	POET
EDNA ST. VINCENT MILLAY	POET
KENNETH L. ROBERTS	AUTHOR
HIRAM S. MAXIM	INVENTOR
LILLIAN NORDICA	OPERA SINGER

CAPITAL CITY	AUGUSTA
POPULATION	1,274,923 40TH LARGEST STATE
ENTERED STATEHOOD	MARCH 15, 1830 23RD STATE
BORDER STATE	NEW HAMPSHIRE
HIGHEST POINT	KATAHDIN MOUNTAIN 5,268 FT.
LOWEST POINT	ATLANTIC COAST, SEA LEVEL
TOPOGRAPHY	APPALACHIAN MOUNTAINS EXTEND THROUGH STATE, WESTERN BOARDERS HAVE RUGGED TERRAIN, LONG SAND BEACHES ON SOUTHERN COAST, NORTHERN COAST MAINLY ROCKY PROMOTORIES, PENNINSULAR, FJORDS
AREA	30865 SQUARE MILES – 39TH LAND SIZE 4523 SQUARE MILES – 39TH WATER SIZE 228 MILES OF COASTLINE – 12TH IN SIZE 3428 MILES SHORELINE – 4TH IN SIZE

ECONOMY

AGRICULTURE	SEAFOOD, POULTRY & EGGS, POTATOES, DAIRY PRODUCTS, CATTLE, BLUEBERRIES, APPLES
INDUSTRY	PAPER, LUMBER/WOOD PRODUCTS, ELECTRIC EQUIPMENT, FOOD PROCESSING, LEATHER PRODUCTS, TEXTILES, TOURISM

- Joshua L. Chamberlain born in Brewer received the only battlefield promotion to General during the Civil War. He was also the last Civil War soldier to die of wounds incurred in the War.
- Approximately 40 million pounds (nearly 90 percent) of the nation's lobster supply is caught off the coast of Maine.
- West Quoddy Head is the easterly point in the United States.
- 90% of the country's toothpick supply is produced in Maine.
- Senator Margaret Chase Smith stood up in the senate and gave the famous Declaration of Conscious speech, speaking out against the McCarthy era. Senator Smith was the first female presidential candidate.
- Water is Maine's history and economy. It produces more canoes than any other state, but also produced the first atomic submarine (THE SWORDFISH), and the first ship built in the western hemisphere, THE VIRGINIA, was launched in 1607.

MARYLAND

MARYLAND

Nickname: ***THE OLD LINE STATE***

FLAG

CAR LICENSE PLATE

Baltimore Oriole
Icterus galbula

Black-eyed susan
Rudbeckia hirta

White oak
Fagaceae Quercus alba

FAMOUS MARYLANDERS

Billie Holiday	Singer
Clara Barton	Founder of the Red Cross
Leon Uris	Author
James Rumsey	Inventor
Harriet Tubman	Abolitionist
Francis Scott Key	Lawyer, Poet
George (Babe) Ruth	Baseball Player
Benjamin Banneker	Mathematician
Frederick Douglass	Social Reformer
Thurgood Marshall	Supreme Court Justice
Samuel Chase	Supreme Court Justice
Charles Carroll	Revolutionary Leader,

CAPITAL CITY	Annapolis
POPULATION	5,296,486 19TH Largest State
ENTERED STATEHOOD	April 28, 1788 7TH State
BORDER STATE	Delaware, Pennsylvania, Virginia, West Virginia
HIGHEST POINT	Backbone Mountain 3,360 ft.
LOWEST POINT	Bloody Point Hole, 174 Ft. Below sea level
TOPOGRAPHY	Eastern shore of Coastal Plain & Maryland Main of coastal plain, piedmont plateau & the blue ridge, separated by the Chesapeake Bay
AREA	9775 SQ. MILES – 42ND LAND SIZE 2633 SQ. MILES – 42ND WATER SIZE 31 MILES OF COASTLINE – 18TH IN SIZE 3190 MILES SHORELINE – 9TH IN SIZE
ECONOMY	
AGRICULTURE	Seafood, poultry & eggs, Dairy products, Nursery stock, cattle, soybeans, corn
INDUSTRY	Electric Equipment, food processing, Chemical products, printing & publishing, Transportation equipment, machinery, Primary metals, coal, tourism

- Babe Ruth, the Sultan of Swat, was born in Baltimore. Other Major League Ball players born in Maryland include Cal Ripken, Jr., Billy Ripken, Lefty Grove, Frank (Home Run) Baker, Harold Baines, Al Kaline, Denny Neagle, and Jimmie Foxx.
- America's national anthem was written by Francis Scott Key a Maryland lawyer, on September 14, 1814 while watching the bombardment of Fort McHenry in Baltimore Harbor.
- September 14, 1975, Elizabeth Ann Seton of Emmitsburg was canonized, becoming the first native-born American to be so honored. She formed the religious community the Sisters of Charity.
- The Methodist Church of America was formally organized in 1784 at Perry Hall.
- On the morning of August 10, 1813, residents of Saint Michaels having been forewarned of a British attack hoisted lanterns to the masts of ships & in the tops of the trees. The height of light caused cannons to overshoot the town. Only one house was struck and is now known as the "Cannonball House."
- The Basilica of the Assumption of the Blessed Virgin Mary is considered a masterpiece and one of the finest 19th century buildings in the world. The basilica is the first cathedral in the United States.

MASSACHUSETTS

MASSACHUSETTS

Nickname: **THE BAY STATE**

FLAG

CAR LICENSE PLATE

Black-capped Chickadee
Penthestes atricapillus

American elm
Ulmaceae Ulmus Americana

Trailing-Arbutus
Epigaea repens

CAPITAL CITY	BOSTON
POPULATION	6,349,097 13TH IN SIZE
ENTERED STATEHOOD	FEBRUARY 6, 1788 6TH STATE
BORDER STATE	CONNECTICUT, NEW HAMPSHIRE, NEW YORK, RHODE ISLAND, VERMONT
HIGHEST POINT	MT. GREYLOCK, 3491 FT
LOWEST POINT	ATLANTIC COAST, SEA LEVEL
AREA	7838 SQ. MILES, 44TH IN LAND SIZE 2717 SQ. MILES 45TH IN WATER SIZE 192 MILES COASTLINE 17TH IN SIZE 1519 MILES SHORELINE, 10TH IN SIZE
TOPOGRAPHY	JAGGED INDENTED COAST AROUND CAPE COD, FLATLAND YEILDS TO STONY UPLAND PASTURES NEAR CENTRAL REGION AND GENTILE HILL COUNTRY IN WEST, WEST IS ROCKY, SANDY AND NOT FERTILE
ECONOMY	
AGRICULTURE	Seafood, Nursery Stock, Dairy Products, Cranberries, Vegetables
IINDUSTRY	Machinery, Electric Equipment Scientific instruments, Printing & Publishing, Tourism

FAMOUS BAY STATERS

John Adams	U.S. President
John Q. Adams	U.S. President
Paul Revere	Patriot, Silversmith
William C. Bryant	Poet, Editor
John Kennedy	U.S. President
George H.W. Bush	U.S. President
Emily E. Dickinson	Poet
Ralph W. Emerson	Poet, Essayist
Louisa M. Alcott	Author
Nathaniel Hawthorne	Author
Winslow Homer	Painter
James Whistler	Artist
Henry Cabot Lodge	Author, Public Official
Susan B. Anthony	Reformer
Bette Davis	Actress
Edgar Allan Poe	Writer
Benjamin Franklin	Scientist, Public Official, Diplomat
John Hancock	Merchant, Public Official
Charles Bulfinch	Architect
Samuel B. Morese	Inventor, Artist
Jack Lemmon	Actor
Luther Burbank	Horticulturis

- 552 original documents pertaining to the Salem witch trials of 1692 have been preserved and are still stored by the Peabody Essex Museum.
- There is a house in Rockport built entirely of newspaper
- The visible portion of Plymouth Rock is a lumpy fragment of glacial moraine about the size of a coffee table, with the date 1620 cut into its surface. After being broken, dragged about the town of Plymouth by ox teams used to inspire Revolutionaries, and reverently gouged and scraped by 19th-century souvenir hunters, it is now at rest near the head of Plymouth Harbor.
- Harvard was the first college established in North America. Harvard was founded in 1636. Because of Harvard's size, there is no universal mailing address that will work for every office at the University
- The Boston University Bridge on Commonwealth Avenue in Boston is the only place in the world where a boat can sail under a train driving under a car driving under an airplane.
- The USS Constitution 'Old Ironsides', the oldest fully commissioned vessel in the US Navy is permanently berthed at Charlestown Navy Yard. Since 1897, the ship has been overhauled several times in Dry Dock 1.

MICHIGAN

Nickname: **THE WOLVERINE STATE**

FLAG

CAR LICENSE PLATE

AMERICAN ROBIN
Turdus migratorius

Apple Blossom
Pyrus coronaria

Eastern white pine
Pinaceae Pinus strobes

FAMOUS MICHIGANIANS, MICHIGANDERS OR MICHIGANITTES

EDNA FERBER	Author
W. K. KELLOGG	Businessman
CHARLES A. LINDBERGH	Aviator
GLENN T. SEABORG	Chemist
RALPH J. BUNCHE	Diplomat
J. O. WOOLLISCROFT	Physician
HENRY FORD	Industrialist, Philanthropistt
AVERY BRUNDAGE	Businessman, Sportsman

CAPITAL CITY	LANSING
POPULATION	9, 938, 44 8TH LARGEST STATE
ENTERED STATEHOOD	JANUARY 26, 1837 26TH STATE
BORDER STATE	ILLINOIS, INDIANA, MINNESOTA, OHIO, WISCONSIN MISSISSIPPI, TENNESSEE
HIGHEST POINT	MT. ARVON, 1900 FT.
LOWEST POINT	SHORE OF LAKE ERIE, 572 FT
TOPOGRAPHY	LOW ROLLING HILLS GIVE WAY TO NORTHERN TABLELAND OF HILLY BELTS IN THE LOWER PENNINSULA; UPPER PENNINSULA IS LEVEL IN THE EAST WITH SWAMPY AREAS, THE WESTERN REGION IS HIGHER AND MORE RUGGED
AREA	56,809 SQUARE MILES – 11TH LAND SIZE 40,001 SQ. MILES – 22ND WATER SIZE
ECONOMY	
AGRICULTURE	DAIRY PRODUCTS, APPLES, BLUEBERRIES, CATTLE, VEGETABLES, HOGS, CORN, NURSERY STOCK, SOYBEANS
INDUSTRY	MOTOR VEHICLES & PARTS, MACHINERY, FABRICATED METAL PRODUCTS, FOOD PROCESSING, CHEMICAL PRODUCTS, MINING, TOURISM

- The Packard Motor Car Company in Detroit manufactured the first air-conditioned car in 1939.
- Michigan State University was founded in 1855 as the nation's first land-grant university and served as the prototype for 69 land-grant institutions later established under the Morrill Act of 1862. It was the first institution of higher learning in the nation to teach scientific agriculture.
- The Mackinac Bridge is one of the longest suspension bridges in the world. Connecting the upper and lower peninsulas of Michigan, it spans 5 miles over the Straits of Mackinac, which is where Lake Michigan and Lake Huron meet. The Mighty Mac took 3 years to complete and was opened to traffic in 1957.
- Michigan is the only place in The world with a floating post office. The J.W. Westcott II is the only boat in the world that delivers mail to ships while they are still underway. They have been operating for 125 years.
- Michigan is the only state that touches four of the five Great Lakes.
- The first auto traffic tunnel built between two nations was the mile-long Detroit-Windsor tunnel under the Detroit River.

MINNESOTA

MINNESOTA

Nickname: ***THE NORTH STAR STATE***

FLAG

CAR LICENSE PLATE

Red pine
Pinaceae Pinus resinosa

Common Loon
Gavia immer

Pink and white lady's-slipper
Cypripedium reginae

FAMOUS MINNESOTANS

FRANCIS S. FITGERALD	Author
JUDY GARLAND	Actress, Singer
J. P. GETTY	Businessman
GARRISON KEILLOR	Humorist
SINCLAIR LEWIS	Author
CHARLES MAYO	Physician
WILLIAM MAYO	Physician
CHARLES M. SCHULZ	Cartoonist
HAROLD E. STASSEN	Pulic Official
DEWITT WALLACE	Plublisher
W.L. WOOLLISCROFT	Businessman
JAMES E. FRASER	Sculptor

CAPITAL CITY	ST. PAUL
POPULATION	4, 919, 479, 21ST LARGEST STATE
ENTERED STATEHOOD	MAY 11, 1858, 32nd STATEE
BORDER STATE	IOWA, MICHIGAN, NORTH DAKOTA, SOUTH DAKOTA, WISCONSIN
HIGHEST POINT	EAGLE MOUNTAIN, 2,301 FT.
LOWEST POINT	SHORE OF LAKE SUPERIOR 602 FT.
TOPOGRAPHY	CENTRAL HILL AND LAKE REGION COVERING APPROXIMATELY HALF THE STATE, TO THE NORTHEAST ROCKY RIDGES AND DEEP LAKES, TO THE NORTHWEST, FLAT PLAINS, TO THE SOUTH, ROLLING PLAINS AND DEEP RIVER VALLEYS
AREA	79,617 SQ. MILES- 12TH IN LAND SIZE 7326 SQ, MILES – 14TH WATER SIZE
ECONOMY	
AGRICULTURE	DAIRY PRODUCTS, CORN, CATTLE, SOYBEANS, HOGS, WHEAT, TURKEYS
INDUSTRY	MACHINERY, FOOD PROCESSING, PRINTING & PUBLISHING, FABRICATED METAL PRODUCTS, ELECTRIC EQUIP-MENT, MINING, TOURISM

- The Mall of America in Bloomington is the size of 78 football fields --- 9.5 million square feet.
- Minnesota Inventions: Masking and Scotch tape, Wheaties cereal, Bisquick, HMOs, the bundt pan, Aveda beauty products, and Green Giant vegetables
- The St. Lawrence Seaway opened in 1959 allowing oceangoing ships to reach Duluth.
- Minneapolis' famed skyway system connecting 52 blocks (nearly five miles) of downtown makes it possible to live, eat, work and shop without going outside.
- Minneapolis has more golfers per capita than any other city in the country.
- The first open heart surgery and the first bone marrow transplant in the United States were done at the University of Minnesota.
- Rollerblades were the first commercially successful in-line Roller Skates. Minnesota students Scott and Brennan Olson invented them in 1980, when they were looking for a way to practice Hockey during the off-season. Their design was an ice hockey boot with 3 inline wheels instead of a blade.
- In 1898, the Kensington Rune stone was found on the farm of Olaf Ohman, near Alexandria. The Kensington Rune stone carvings allegedly tell of a journey of a band of Vikings in 1362.

MISSISSIPPI

MISSISSIPPI

Nickname: **THE MAGNOLIA STATE**

FLAG

CAR LICENSE PLATE

Southern magnolia
Magnoliaceae Magnolia grandiflora

Mockingbird
Mimus polyglottos

Magnolia
Magnolia grandiflora

FAMOUS MISSISSIPPIANS

WILLIAM C. FAULKNER	AUTHOR
JAMES E. JONES	ACTOR
ELVIS PRESLEY	ENTERTAINER
TENNESSEE WILLIAMS	PLAYWRIGHT
THEODORE BILBO	PUBLIC OFFICIAL
LEONTYNE PRICE	OPERA SINGER

CAPITAL CITY	Jackson
POPULATION	2, 844, 658, 31ST Largest State
ENTERED STATEHOOD	Dec. 10, 1817, 20TH State
BORDER STATE	Alabama, Arkansas, Louisiana Tennessee
HIGHEST POINT	Woodall Mountain, 806 Ft.
LOWEST POINT	Gulf of Mexico/Sea Level
TOPOGRAPHY	Low, fertile delta between Yazoo & Mississippi Rivers, bluffs stretching around delta boarders, sand gulf coastal terraces followed by piney woods and prairie, rugged high sandy hills in extreme northeast, followed by black prairie belt, Pontotoc ridge and flat woods into the north central highlands
AREA	46,914 Sq. Miles – 32ND Land size 1520 SQ. Miles – 31ST Water size 53 Miles of Coastline - 25TH in size 359 Miles of Shoreline-18th in size
ECONOMY	
AGRICULTURE	Cotton, poultry, cattle, catfish soybeans, dairy products, rice
INDUSTRY	Apparel, furniture, lumber &wood Products, food, processing, electrical machinery, transportation equipment

- In 1902 while on a hunting expedition in Sharkey County, President Theodore (Teddy) Roosevelt refused to shoot a captured bear. This act resulted in the creation of the world-famous teddy bear.
- Burnita Shelton Mathews of Hazlehurst was the first woman federal judge in the United States and served in Washington, the District of Columbia.
- The rarest of North American cranes lives in Mississippi in the grassy savannas of Jackson County. The Mississippi Sand hill Crane stands about 44 inches tall and has an eight-foot wingspan.
- In 1834 Captain Isaac Ross, whose plantation was in Lorman, freed his slaves and arranged for them to be sent to Africa, where they founded the country of Liberia. Recently, representatives of Liberia visited Lorman and placed a stone at the Captain's gravesite in honor of his kindness.
- The Natchez Trace Parkway, named an All American Road by the federal government, extends from Natchez to just south of Nashville, Tennessee. The Trace began as an Indian trail more than 8,000 years ago.
- The Vicksburg National Cemetery is the second largest national cemetery in the country. Arlington National Cemetery is the largest.
- This was a one-crop state (cotton) before the arrival of the boll weevil in 1907. Manufacturing has taken over the lead in the state's economy, as the largest producer of upholstered furniture.

MISSOURI

MISSOURI

Nickname: ***THE SHOW ME STATE***

FLAG

CAR LICENSE PLATE

Bluebird
Sialia sialis

Hawthorn
Crataegus

Flowering dogwood
Cornaceae Cornus florida

FAMOUS MISSOURIANS

Josephine Baker	Entertainer
Thomas H. Benton	Painter
Dale Carnegie	Author, Teacher of Public Speaking
George W. Carver	Agronomist, Chemist
Samuel L. Clemens	(Mark Twain) Humorist, Author
Walter L. Cronkite, Jr.	Journalist
Ginger Rogers	Actress, Dancer
T.S. Eliot	Poet, Critic
J.C. Penney	Merchant
J.J. Pershing	Soldier
Harry S. Truman	U.S. President

CAPITAL CITY	Jefferson City
POPULATION	5,595,211 17TH Largest State
ENTERED STATEHOOD	Aug. 10, 1821 24TH State
BORDER STATE	Arkansas, Illinois, Iowa, Kansas, Kentucky, Nebraska, Oklahoma, Tennessee
HIGHEST POINT	Taum Lake Mts. 1,772 FT.
LOWEST POINT	Saint Francis River, 230 FT.
TOPOGRAPHY	Rolling hills, open fertile plains and well-watered prairie north of the Missouri river, south of the river land is rough and hilly with deep narrow valleys, alluvial plain in the southeast, low elevations in the west.
AREA	68,898 SQ. miles-21ST Land size 811 SQ. Miles – 18TH Water size
ECONOMY	
AGRICULTURE	Cattle, Soybeans, Hogs, Dairy Products, corn, Poultry & eggs.
INDUSTRY	Transportation Equipment, Food processing, chemical products, electric equipment, fabricated metal products.

- The most destructive tornado on record occurred in Annapolis. In 3 hours, it tore through the town on March 18, 1925 leaving a 980-foot wide trail of demolished buildings, uprooted trees, and overturned cars. It left 823 people dead and almost 3,000 injured.
- At the St. Louis World's Fair in 1904, the ice cream cone was invented. An ice cream vendor ran out of cups and asked a waffle vendor to help by rolling up waffles to hold ice cream.
- Jefferson National Expansion Memorial consists of the Gateway Arch, the Museum of Westward Expansion, and St. Louis' Old Courthouse. During a nationwide competition in 1947-48, architect Eero Saarinen's inspired design for a 630-foot stainless steel arch was chosen as a perfect monument to the spirit of the western pioneers. Construction of the Arch began in 1963 and was completed on October 28, 1965.The Arch has foundations sunken 60 feet into the ground, and is built to withstand earthquakes and high winds. It sways up to one inch in a 20 mph wind, and is built to sway up to 18 inches.
- In 1889, Aunt Jemima pancake flour, invented at St. Joseph, Missouri, was the first self-rising flour for pancakes and the first ready-mix food ever to be introduced commercially.
- The most powerful earthquake to strike the United States occurred in 1811, centered in New Madrid, Missouri. The quake shook more than one million square miles, and was felt as far as 1,000 miles away.
- Madonna of the Trail" monument in Lexington tells the story of the brave women who helped conquer the west and is one of 12 placed in every state crossed by the National Old Trails Road, the route of early settlers from Maryland to California.

M O N T A N A

MONTANA

Nickname:
THE TREASURE STATE

FLAG

CAR LICENSE PLATE

Ponderosa pine
Pinaceae Pinus ponderosa

Western Meadowlark
Sturnella neglecta

Bitterroot
Lewisia rediviva

FAMOUS MONTANANS

Gary Cooper	Actor
Chet Huntley	Journalist, Commentator
Myrna Loy	Actress
Jeannette Rankin	Suffragist, Public Official
Washakie	Indian Leader
Kevin Ancell	Guide

CAPITAL CITY	HELENA
POPULATION	902,195, 44TH LARGEST STATE
ENTERED STATEHOOD	NOV. 8, 1889, 41ST STATE
BORDER STATE	IDAHO, NORTH DAKOTA, SOUTH DAKOTA, WYOMING
HIGHEST POINT	GRANITE PEAK, 12,799 FT.
LOWEST POINT	KOOTENA RIVER, 1800 FT.
TOPOGRAPHY	ROCKY MOUNTAINS IN THE WESTERN THIRD OF THE STATE, EASTERN TWO-THIRDS GENTLY ROLLING NORTHERN GREAT PLAINS
AREA	145,556 SQ. MILES – 4TH LAND SIZE 1490 SQ. MILES – 4TH IN WATER SIZE
ECONOMY	
AGRICULTURE	CATTLE, WHEAT, BARLEY, SUGAR BEETS, HAY, HOGS
INDUSTRY	MINING, LUMBER & WOOD PRODUCTS, FOOD PROCESSING, TOURISM

- Montana has the largest migratory elk herd in the nation. The average square mile of land contains 1.4 elk, 1.4 pronghorn antelope, and 3.3 deer.
- The state boasts the largest breeding population of trumpeter swans in the lower United States. The Freezeout Lake Wildlife Management Area contains as many as 300,000 snow geese and 10,000 tundra swans during migration. At Bowdoin National Wildlife Refuge, it is possible to see up to 1,700 nesting pelicans. Every spring nearly 10,000 white pelicans with a wingspan of nine feet migrate from the Gulf of Mexico to Medicine Lake in northeastern Montana
- The Montana Yogo Sapphire is the only North American gem to be included in the Crown Jewels of England.
- 46 out of Montana's 56 counties are considered "frontier counties" with an average population of 6 or fewer people per square mile. In Montana the elk, deer and antelope populations outnumber the humans
- At Egg Mountain near Choteau dinosaur eggs have been discovered supporting the theory some dinosaurs were more like mammals and birds than like reptiles.
- Montana is the only state with a triple divide allowing water to flow into the Pacific, Atlantic, and Hudson Bay. This phenomenon occurs at Triple Divide Peak in Glacier National Park. Flathead Lake in northwest Montana contains over 200 square miles of water and 185 miles of shoreline. It is considered the largest natural freshwater lake in the west.
- The first luge run in North America was built at Lolo Hot Springs on Lolo Pass in 1965.
- Virginia City was founded in 1863 and is considered to be the most complete original town of its kind in the United States.
- Just south of Billings, Lt. Col. George Armstrong Custer and his troops made their last stand. Little Bighorn Battlefield National Monument features the Plains Indians and United States military involved in the historic battle.

NEBRASKA

NEBRASKA

Nickname: ***THE CORNHUSKER STATE***

FLAG

CAR LICENSE PLATE

Western Meadowlark
Sturnella neglecta

Goldenrod
Soldiago gigantea

Cottonwood
Salicaceae Populus deltoides

CAPITAL CITY	LINCOLN
POPULATION	1,711,263 38TH LARGEST STATE
ENTERED STATEHOOD	MARCH 1, 1867, 37TH STATE
BORDER STATE	COLORADO, IOWA, KANSAS, MISSOURI, SOUTH DAKOTA, WYOMING
HIGHEST POINT	PANORAMA POINT, 5,424 FT.
LOWEST POINT	MISSOURI RIVER, 480 FT.
TOPOGRAPHY	Fertile PLAINS OF THE CENTRAL LOWLAND IN THE EASTERN THIRD RISING TO THE GREAT PLAINS AND HILL COUNTRY OF THE NORTH CENTRAL AND NORTHWEST
AREA	76, SQ. MILES – 16TH LAND SIZE 481 SQ. MILES- 15TH WATER SIZE
ECONOMY	
AGRICULTURE	CATTLE, CORN, HOGS, SOYBEANS, WHEAT, SORGHUM,
INDUSTRY	FOOD PROCESSING, MACHINERY, ELECTRIC EQUIPMENT, PRINTING AND PUBLISHING

FAMOUS NEBRASKANSS

Gerald Ford	U.S. President
Fred Astaire	dancer, actor,
Max Baer	Boxer
George Beadle	geneticist,
Marlon Brando	actor,
Warren Buffett	investor
Montgomery Clift	actor
James Coburn	actor
Sandy Dennis	actress
Mignon Eberhart	author
Henry Fonda	actor
Jay W. Forrester	inventor
Bob Gibson	baseball player,
Hoot Gibson	actor
Susette La Flesche	artist
Malcolm X	civil rights dvocate
Nick Nolte	actor,
Roscoe Pound	educator,
Red Cloud	Indian rights advocate leader
Mari Sandoz	author,
Standing Bear	Indian rights advocate leader
Darryl F. Zanuck	film producer,

- The Lied Jungle located in Omaha is the world's largest indoor rain forest.
- Nebraska is the birthplace of the Reuben sandwich.
- Nebraska has the U.S.'s largest aquifer (underground lake/water supply), the Ogallala aquifer.
- Nebraska is the only state in the union with a unicameral (one-house) legislature.
- Nebraska's Chimney rock was the most often mentioned landmark in journal entries by travelers on the Oregon Trail.
- Marlon Brando's mother gave Henry Fonda acting lessons at the Omaha Community Playhouse.
- Mutual of Omaha Corporate headquarters is a public building built with 7 floors underground.
- The largest porch swing in the world is located in Hebron, Nebraska and it can sit 25 adults.
- The world's largest hand-planted forest is Halsey National Forrest near Thedford, Nebraska
- Father Edward Flanagan founded Boys Town in Omaha, Nebraska in 1917.

NEVADA

Nickname: **THE SILVER STATE**

FLAG

CAR LICENSE PLATE

Bristlecone pine
Pinaceae Pinus aristata

Mountain Bluebird
Sialia currucoides

Sagebrush
Artemisia tridentata

FAMOUS NEVADANS

Ben Alexander	actor,
Andre Agassi	tennis player,
Abby Dalton	actress,
Harry M. Reid	politician
Paul Laxalt	politician,
Sarah H. Winnemucca	author, Paiute interpreter, peacemaker
Jack Wilson	Piute Indian prophet
Edna Purviance	actress,
Jack Kramer	tennis player,
Thelma Pat Nixon	First Lady,

CAPITAL CITY	CARSON CITY
POPULATION	1,998,257 35TH LARGEST STATE
ENTERED STATEHOOD	OCTOBER 31, 1864 36TH STATE
BORDER STATE	ARIZONA, CALIFORNIA, IDAHO, OREGON, UTAH
HIGHEST POINT	BOUNDARY PARK, 13,143 FT.
LOWEST POINT	COLORADO RIVER, 470 FT.
TOPOGRAPHY	RUGGED NORTH-SOUTH MOUNTAIN RANGE, SOUTHERN AREA IS WITHIN THE MOJAVE DESERT WITH THE COLORADO RIVER CANYON
AREA	109,806 SQ. MILES – 7TH LAND SIZE 761 SQ. MILES – 7TH WATER SIZE
ECONOMY	
AGRICULTURE	CATTLE, HAY, DAIRY PRODUCTS, POTATOES
INDUSTRY	TOURISM, MINING, MACHINERY, PRINTING AND PUBLISHING, FOOD PROCESSING, ELECTRIC EQUIPMENT

- In 1899, Charles Fey invented a slot machine named the Liberty Bell. The device became the model for all slots to follow.
- Bugsy Siegel named his Las Vegas casino “The Flamingo” for the long legs of his showgirl sweetheart, Virginia Hill.
- There were 16,067 slots in Nevada in 1960. In 1999, Nevada had 205,726 slot machines, one for every 10 residents.
- In 1931, the Pair-O-Dice Club was the first casino to open on Highway 91, the future Las Vegas Strip.
- Once the highest concrete dam in the world, Hoover Dam offers guided tours and a museum of artifacts of the construction and its workers.
- In Death Valley, the Kangaroo Rat can live its entire life without drinking a drop of liquid.
- In Tonopah, the young Jack Dempsey was once the bartender and the bouncer at the still popular Mispah Hotel and Casino. Famous lawman and folk hero Wyatt Earp once kept the peace in the town.
- Austin’s oldest church, St. Augustine, requires the establishment’s bells in the tower to be rung by pulling a rope located in the men’s restroom.
- Most of the state is desert but the Sierra Nevada mountain range near Reno and the Ruby Mountains near Elko has snow for half the year.
- The longest running show in Las Vegas is the Follies Bergere at the Tropicana Hotel and Casino. It opened in 1959. The production numbers in “Showgirls” were written specifically for the Paul Verhoeven film and shot in the Horizon Hotel at Lake Tahoe. The bulk of the movie used locations located at the Luxor and the Forum Shops at Caesars.
- Nevada is the largest gold-producing state in the nation. It is second in the world behind South Africa.
- Hoover Dam, the largest single public works project in the history of the United States, contains 3.25 million cubic yards of concrete, which is enough to pave a two-lane highway from San Francisco to New York. The dam face was used in an amazing stunt for Roland Emerich’s “Universal Soldier” and has been seen in such films as “Viva Las Vegas” and “Fools Rush In.”
- Camels were used as pack animals in Nevada as late as 1870.

NEW HAMPSHIRE

NEW HAMPSHIRE

Nickname: ***THE GRANITE STATE***

FLAG

CAR LICENSE PLATE

Purple Finch
Carpodacus purpureus

PURPLE LILAC
Syringa vulgaris

Paper birch
Betulaceae Betula papyrifera

FAMOUS NEW HAMPSHIREITES

Daniel Webster	Politician, Statesman
Franklin Pierce	U.S. President
Alan Shepard	Astronaut
Christa Mcauliffe	Teacher
Horace Greeley	Journalist

CAPITAL CITY	CONCOARD
POPULATION	4,447,100 23RD LARGEST STATE
ENTERED STATEHOOD	JUNE 21, 1788 9TH STATE
BORDER STATE	MAINE, MASSACHUSETTS, VERMONT
HIGHEST POINT	MT. WASHINGTON, 6,288 FT
LOWEST POINT	ATLANTIC COAST, SEA LEVEL
TOPOGRAPHY	LOW ROLLING COAST FOLLOWED BY COUNTLESS HILLS AND MOUNTAINS RISING OUT OF A CENTRAL PLATEAU
AREA	8969 SQ. MILES – 46TH LAND SIZE 382 SQ. MILESS – 44TH WATER SIZE 13 MILES COASTLINE – 45TH 131 MILES SHORELINE – 22ND IN SIZE
ECONOMY	
AGRICULTURE	DAIRY PRODUCTS, NURSERY STOCK, CATTLE, APPLES, EGGS
INDUSTRY	MACHINERY, ELECTRIC EQUIPMENT, RUBBER AND PLASTIC PRODUCTS, TOURISM

- Of the thirteen original colonies, New Hampshire was the first to declare its independence from Mother England -- a full six months before the Declaration of Independence was signed.
- The highest wind speed recorded at ground level was at Mt. Washington, on April 12, 1934. The winds were three times as fast as those in most hurricanes.
- New Hampshire's present constitution was adopted in 1784; it is the second oldest in the country.
- On December 30, 1828, about 400 mill girls walked out of the Dover Cotton Factory enacting the first women's strike in the United States.
- Augustus Saint-Gaudens from Cornish was the first sculptor to design an American coin. His commission became fraught with difficulties related to Saint-Gaudens' desire for high relief relative to the demands of mass production and use.
- America's Stonehenge is a 4000 year old megalithic (stone constructed) site located on Mystery Hill in Salem and presently serves as a leisurely, educational tour for the whole family.
- The Memorial Bell Tower at Cathedral of the Pines in Rindge has four bronze bas-reliefs designed by Norman Rockwell. The bell tower is specifically dedicated to women — military and civilian — who died serving their country.
- The Bavarian-style hamlet of Merrimack is home to the famous eight-horse hitch, the Clydesdales maintained by the Anheuser-Busch Brewery.
- The Belknap Mill built at Laconia in 1823 is the oldest unaltered brick knitting mill in America.
- The Blue Ghost of Wolfeboro is the U.S. Mail Boat for Lake Winnipesaukee. It makes a daily 60-mile loop delivering mail to 30 stops at camps and islands around the lake.
- The granite profile "Old Man of the Mountain" is one of the most famous natural landmarks in the state. The Old Man's head measures 40 feet from chin to forehead and is made up of five ledges. Nature carved this profile thousands of years ago. The natural sculpture is 1,200 feet above Echo Lake.

NEW JERSEY

NEW JERSEY

Nickname: **THE GARDEN STATE**

FLAG

CAR LICENSE PLATE

Eastern Goldfinch
Carduelis tristis

Violet
Viola sororia

Northern red oak
Fagaceae Quercus rubra

FAMOUS NEW JERSEYITES

GROVER CLEVELAND	U.S. PRESIDENT
JACK NICHOLSON	ACTOR
QUEEN LATIFA	ACTOR
FRANK SINATRA	ENTERTAINER
BRUCE SPRINGSTEEN	MUSICIAN
BON JOVI	MUSICIAN
JUDY BLUME	FIGURE SKATER
WHITNEY HOUSTON	ENTERTAINER

CAPITAL CITY	TRENTON
POPULATION	8,414, 350 9TH LARGEST STATE
ENTERED STATEHOOD	DEC. 18, 1787 3RD STATE
BORDER STATE	DELAWARE, NEW YORK, PENNSYLVANIA
HIGHEST POINT	HIGH POINT, 1803 FT.
LOWEST POINT	ATLANTIC COAST, SEA LEVEL
TOPOGRAPHY	APPALACHIAN VALLEY IN THE NORTHWEST HAS HIGHEST ELEVATIONS: APPALACHIAN Highlands, flat topped northwest-southwest mountain ranges, piedmont plateau, low plains broken by high ridges, coastal plain, covering three-fifths of the state in southeast, gradually rises to gentle slopes
AREA	7419 SQ. MILES – 47H LAND SIZE 1303 SQ. MILES – 46TH WATER SIZE 130 MILES OF COASTLINE – 27TH IN SIZE 1,792 MILES SHORELINE – 13TH IN SIZE
ECONOMY	
AGRICULTURE	NURSERY STOCK, HORSES, VEGETABLES, FRUITS AND NUTS, SEAFOOD, DAIRY PRODUCTS
INDUSTRY	CHEMICAL PRODUCTS, FOOD PROCESSING, ELECTRIC EQUIPMENT, PRINTING AND PUBLISHING, TOURISM

- New Jersey has the highest population density in the U.S. An average 1,030 people per sq. mi., which is 13 times the national average.
- New Jersey has the highest percent urban population in the U.S. with about 90% of the people living in an urban area.
- New Jersey has the most dense system of highways and railroads in the U.S.
- In order to meet the increasing demand for his wire rope John Roebling opened a factory in Trenton, New Jersey in 1848. John Roebling, along with his two sons, Washington and Ferdinand, built a suspension bridge across the gorge of the Niagara River. They then built the Brooklyn Bridge plus many other suspension bridges in the United States.
- New Jersey is a major seaport state with the largest seaport in the U.S. located in Elizabeth.
- The light bulb, phonograph (record player), motion picture projector were invented by Thomas Edison in his Menlo Park laboratory.
- Atlantic City has the longest boardwalk in the world.

NEW MEXICO

Nickname: **LAND OF ENCHANTMENT**

FLAG

CAR LICENSE PLATE

Pinyon pine
Pinaceae Pinus edulis

ROADRUNNER
Geococcyx californianus

Yucca flower
Yucca glauca

FAMOUS NEW MEXICANS

Bruce Cabot	actor	**Mangus Coloradas**	apache leader
Edward Condon	physicist	**Robert Crichton**	author
John Denver	singer	**Pete Domenici**	senator
Sid Gutierrez	astronaut	**William Hanna**	animator
Conrad Hilton	hotel executive	**Peter Hurd**	artist
John Madden	sportscaster	**Demi Moore**	actress
Al Unser	auto racer	**Bobby Unser**	auto racer
Victorio	Apache chief	**Thomas Weaver**	anthropologist, author

CAPITAL CITY	Santa Fe
POPULATION	1,819, 046 36TH Largest State
ENTERED STATEHOOD	JAN. 6, 1912 47TH State
BORDER STATE	Arizona, Colorado, Oklahoma, Texas, Utah
HIGHEST POINT	Wheeler Peak, 13,161 FT.
LOWEST POINT	Red Bluff Lake, 2,817 FT.
TOPOGRAPHY	Eastern third, great plains, central third, Rocky Mountain, western third, High Plateau. 85% of the state is over 4,000 feet in elevation
AREA	121,359 SQ. MILES – 5TH Land size 234 SQ. MILES – 5TH Water size 53 Miles of coastline – 17TH in size 607 Miles shoreline – 19TH in size
ECONOMY	
AGRICULTURE	Cattle, dairy products, hay nursery stock, chilies
INDUSTRY	Electric equipment, petroleum & coal products, food processing, printing & publishing, stone, Glass and clay products, tourism.

- Each October Albuquerque hosts the world's largest international hot air balloon fiesta.
- Lakes and Rivers make up only .002% of the state's total surface area. The lowest water-to-land ratio of all 50 states. Most of New Mexico's lakes are man-made reservoirs. A dam on the Rio Grande formed the Elephant Butte Reservoir the state's largest lake.
- The world's first Atomic Bomb was detonated on July 16, 1945 on the White Sands Testing Range near Alamogordo. North of the impact point, a small placard marks the area known as Trinity Site. The bomb was designed and manufactured in Los Alamos.
- The word "Pueblo" is used to describe a group of people, a town, or an architectural style. There are 19 Pueblo groups that speak 4 distinct languages. The Pueblo people of the southwest have lived in the same location longer than any other culture in the Nation.
- The Navajo, the Nation's largest Native American Group, have a reservation that covers 14 million Acres.
- In some isolated villages, such as Truchas, Chimayo', and Coyote in north-central New Mexico, some descendants of Spanish conquistadors still speak a form of 16th century Spanish used nowhere else in the world today.
- The father of modern rocketry Massachusetts scientist Robert Goddard whom some called a crackpot, came to New Mexico in 1930 to test rocket-ship models. From those humble beginnings, the aerospace industry became one of New Mexico's leading industries.
- Tens of thousands of bats live in the Carlsbad Caverns. The largest chamber is more than 10 football fields long and about 22 stories high.
- Taos Pueblo is located 2 miles north of the city of Taos. It is one of the oldest continuously occupied communities in the United States. People still live in some of its 900-year-old buildings.

NEW YORK

Nickname: **EMPIRE STATE**

FLAG

CAR LICENSE PLATE

Sugar maple
Aceraceae Acer saccharum

Bluebird
Sialia sialis

ROSE
Rosa

FAMOUS NEW YORKERS

Martin Van Buren	U.S. President	**Walt Whitman**	Poet, philosopher
Millard Fillmore	U.S. President	**Kateri Tekakwitha**	Religious figure
Theodore Roosevelt	U.S. President	**Barbra Streisand**	Singer, actress
Franklin D. Roosevelt	U.S. President	**Shenandoah**	Indian leader
Julia Ward Howe	Author, social reformer	**John Rockefeller**	Industrialist, philanthropist
Washington Irving	Author	**Frederic Remington**	Artist
Michael Jordan	Basketball Player	**Lou Gehrig**	Baseball player

CAPITAL CITY	ALBANY
POPULATION	18,976,457, 3RD LARGEST STATE
ENTERED STATEHOOD	JULY 26, 1788, 11TH STATE
BORDER STATE	Connecticut, Massachusetts, New Jersey, Pennsylvania, Rhode Island, Vermont
HIGHEST POINT	MT. MARCY, 5,344 FT.
LOWEST POINT	ATLANDTIC COAST, SEA LEVEL
TOPOGRAPHY	Highest & and most rugged mountains in the northeast Adirondack upland. Saint Lawrence-Champlain lowlands extend from Lake Ontario northeast along the Canadian border; Hudson-Mohawk lowland follows the flows of the rivers north & west; Atlantic coastal plain in the southwest; Appalachian highlands cover half of the state west-ward from the Hudson valley, including the Catskill Mountain Finger Lakes; plateau of Erie-Ontario lowlands
AREA	47,224 SQ. MILES – 27TH LAND SIZE 7251 SQ. MILES – 30TH WATER SIZE 127 MILES COASTLINE – 8TH IN SIZE 1,850 MILES SHORELINE – 13TH IN SIZE
ECONOMY	
AGRICULTURE	Dairy products, cattle & other livestock, vegetables, nursery stock, apples
INDUSTRY	Printing & publishing, scientific instruments, electric equipment, machinery, chemical products, tourism

- A brewer named Matthew Vassar founded Vassar College in Poughkeepsie in 1861.
- In 1979, Vassar students were the first from a private college to be granted permission to study in the People's Republic of China.
- The Fashion Institute of Technology in Manhattan is the only school in the world offering a Bachelor of Science Degree with a Major in Cosmetics and Fragrance Marketing.
- Sam Schapiro began the Kosher wine industry on New York's Lower East side with their famous extra heavy original concord wine in 1899.
- New York City has 722 miles of subway track.
- Oneida has the world's smallest church with the dimensions of 3.5' X 6'.
- The Genesee River is one of the few rivers in the world that flows south to north.
- On July 28, 1945, an Army Air Corps B-25 crashed into the Empire State Building at the 79th floor level.
- European settlers who brought seeds to New York introduced apples in the 1600s.
- Wade Boggs and Cal Ripken Jr. played against each other in Rochester vs. Pawtucket Red Sox in the longest game in baseball history. The game went a total of 33 innings.

NORTH CAROLINA

NORTH CAROLINA

Nickname:
OLD NORTH STATE
OR TAR HEEL STATE

FLAG

CAR LICENSE PLATE

Cardinal
Cardinalis cardinalis

American Dogwood
Cornus florida

Longleaf pine
Pinaceae Pinus palustris

FAMOUS NORTH CAROLINIANS

JAMES K. POLK	U.S. PRESIDENT
ANDREW JOHNSON	U.S. PRESIDENT
BILLY GRAHAM	EVANGILIST
THOMAS WOLFE	AUTHOR
EDWARD R. MURROW	JOURNALIST, BROADCASTER
JACOB JONES	OFFICER

CAPITAL CITY	RALEIGH
POPULATION	8,049,313 11TH LARGEST STATE
ENTERED STATEHOOD	NOVEMBER 21, 1789, 12TH STATE
BORDER STATE	GEORGIA, SOUTH CAROLINA, TENNESSEE, VIRGINIA
HIGHEST POINT	MT. MITCHELL, 6,684 FT.
LOWEST POINT	ATLANTIC COAST, SEA LEVEL
TOPOGRAPHY	COASTAL PLAINS AND TIDEWATER IN TWO-FIFTHS OF STATE, EXTENDING TO THE FALL LINE OF THE RIVERS, PIEDMONT PLATEAU, ANOTHER TWO-FIFTHS OF GENTLE TO RUGGED HILLS, SOUTHERN AAALACHIAN MOUNTAINS CONTAIN BLUE RIDGE AND GREAT SMOKEY MOUNTAINS
AREA	48,718 SQ. MILES, 28TH LAND SIZE 5103 SQ. MILES – 29TH WATER SIZE 301 MILES OF COASTLINE – 10TH IN SIZE 3,375 MILES OF SHORELINE – 7TH IN SIZE
ECONOMY	
AGRICULTURE	POULTRY & EGGS, TOBACCO, HOGS, MILK, NURSERY STOCK, CATTLE, SOYBEANS
INDUSTRY	TOBACCO PRODUCTS, TEXTILE GOODS, CHEMICAL PRODUCS, ELECTRIC EQUIPMENT, MACHINERY, TOURISM

- The University of North Carolina Chapel Hill is the oldest State University in the United States.
- In 1903, the Wright Brothers made the first successful powered flight by man at Kill Devil Hill near Kitty Hawk.
  Whitewater Falls in Transylvania County is the highest waterfall in the eastern United States.
- The first English colony in America was located on Roanoke Island. Walter Raleigh founded it. The colony mysteriously vanished with no trace except for the word "Croatoan" scrawled on a nearby tree.
- The Biltmore Estate in Ashville is America's largest home, and includes a 255-room chateau, an award-winning winery and extensive gardens.
- The first English child born in America was born in Roanoke in 1587. Her name was Virginia Dare.
- Fontana Dam is the tallest dam in the Eastern United States, at 480 feet high.
- Grandfather Mountain, highest peak in the Blue Ridge, is the only private park in the world designated by the United Nations as an International Biosphere Reserve.
- The Mile-High Swinging Bridge near Linville is 5,305 feet above sea level. The bridge actually hangs about 80 feet above the ground.
- Pepsi was invented and first served in New Bern in 1898.
- Arnold Palmer recognized as the player whose aggressive play and winning personality raised golf to national attention, honed his skills on the championship golf team of Wake Forest University.
- The Swiss and German settlement of New Bern was named in honor of the founder's home, Bern, Switzerland. When Bern, Switzerland was founded, it was named by a group of hunters. They named the city for the first animal they came upon on their hunting expedition. It was a bear. "Bern" is the old Germanic word for Bear, and the bear became the symbol of the city. It has been adopted by New Bern, as well.
- White Lake near Elizabethtown is unique in that it has a white sandy bottom and crystal clear waters. It has been labeled as the "Nation's Safest Beach." There are no currents, no tides, no hazardous depressions or real dangers of any kind to swimmers.

NORTH DAKOTA

NORTH DAKOTA

Nickname: **PEACE GARDEN STATE**

American elm
Ulmaceae Ulmus Americana

Western Meadowlark.
TURNELLA NEGLECTA,

Wild Prairie Rose
Rosa arkansana

FAMOUS NORTH DAKOTANS

Elizabeth Bodine	humanitarian
Angie Dickinson	actress,
Ivan Dmitre	artist
John Bernard Flannagan	sculptor,
Dr. Leon O. Jacobson	researcher, educator,
Louis L'Amour	author,
Peggy Lee	singer,
Marquis de Mores	cattleman
Casper Oimoen	skier
Cliff Fido Purpur	hockey player, coach
James Rosenquist	painter,
Eric Sevareid	TV commentator,
Ann Sothern	actress
Edward K. Thompson	editor
Era Bell Thompson	editor
Tommy Tucker	band leader,
Lawrence Welk	band leader, Entertainer,
Phil D. Jackson	basketball player, Coach

CAPITAL CITY	BISMARCK
POPULATION	642.200 47TH LARGEST STATE
ENTERED STATEHOOD	NOVEMBER 2, 1889 39TH STATE
BORDER STATE	MINNESOTA, MONTANA, SOUTH DAKOTA (CANADA TO THE NORTH)
HIGHEST POINT	WHITE BUTTE, 3,506 FT.
LOWEST POINT	RED RIVER, 750 FT.
TOPOGRAPHY	CENTRAL LOWLANDS IN THE EAST COMPRISES THE FLAT RED RIVER VALLEY AND THE ROLLING DRIFT PRARIE; MISSOURI PLATEAU OF THE GREAT PLAINS IN THE WEST
AREA	68,994 SQUARE MILES – 19TH LAND SIZE 1710 SQUARE MILES – 17TH WATER SIZE
ECONOMY	
AGRICULTURE	WHEAT, CATTLE, BARLEY, SUNFLOWERS, MILK, SUGAR BEETS
INDUSTRY	FOOD PROCESSING, MACHINERY, MINING, TOURISM

- The town of Rugby is the geographical center of North America. A rock obelisk about 15 feet tall flanked by poles flying the United States and Canadian flags marks the location.
- Geologically speaking Hillsboro is located in a large, flat, and ancient dried lake bottom surrounded by some of the most fertile farmland in the world.
- Richardton is home to the Abbey Church a Bavarian Romanesque structure. Lofty arches, 52 stained glass windows, 24 paintings of Saints on canvas above the arches, and a huge carved crucifix delineate the impressive interior.
- Sitting Bull Burial State Historic Site located on the western edge of Fort Yates marks the original grave of the Hunkpapa Sioux leader. During the Ghost Dance, unrest of 1890 an attempt was made to arrest him at his home on the Grand River in South Dakota, and a skirmish ensued in which Sitting Bull was killed.
- Only one word is needed to describe Lake Sakakawea country - big. From the massive two-mile long Garrison Dam near Riverdale to the end of Lake Sakakawea near Williston, Lake Sakakawea is nearly 200 miles long with a shoreline of countless bays and inlets that cover 1,600 miles.

OHIO

OHIO

Nickname:
THE BUCKEYE STATE

FLAG

CAR LICENSE PLATE

Cardinal
Cardinalis cardinalis

Scarlet Carnation
Dianthus caryophyllus

Ohio buckeye
Hippocastanaceae Aesculus glabra

FAMOUS OHIOANS

Ulyses S. Grant	U.S. PRESIDENT
Rutherford B. Hayes	U.S. PRESIDENT
James A. Garfield	U.S. PRESIDENT
Benjamin Harrison	U.S. PRESIDENT
William McKinley	U.S. PRESIDENT
William H. Taft	U.S. PRESIDENT
Warren G. Harding	U.S. PRESIDENT
John Glenn	ASTRONAUT
Neil Armstrong	ASTRONAUT
Jesse Owens	OLYMPIAN

CAPITAL CITY	COLUMBUS
POPULATION	11,353,140 7TH LARGEST STATE
ENTERED STATEHOOD	MARCH 1, 1803 17TH STATE
BORDER STATE	INDIANA, KENTUCKY, MICHIGAN, PENNSYLVANIA, WEST VIRGINIA
HIGHEST POINT	CAMPBELL HILL, 1,550 FT.
LOWEST POINT	OHIO RIVR, 433 FT.
TOPOGRAPHY	GENERALLY ROLLING PLAIN, ALLEGHENY PLATEAU LOCATED IN THE EAST; LAKE ERIE PLAINS EXTEND SOUTHWARD, CENTRAL PLAINS IN THE WEST.
AREA	40,953 SQ. MILES – 34TH LAND SIZE 3875 SQ. MILES – 35TH WATER SIZE
ECONOMY	
AGRICULTURE	SOYBEANS, DAIRY PRODUCTS, CORN, TOMATOES, HOGS, CATTLE, POULTRY AND EGGS
INDUSTRY	TRANSPORTATION EQUIPMENT, FABRICATED METAL PRODUCTS, MACHINERY, FOOD PROCESSING, ELECTRIC EQUIPMENT

1. The Y Bridge in Zanesville was first built in 1814 to span the confluence of the Licking and Muskingum Rivers. The current bridge is the fifth construction at the same location. "Ripley's Believe It or Not" proclaimed it the only bridge in the world which you can cross and still be on the same side of the river.
2. Ohio senator John Glenn became the oldest man to venture into outer space. On February 20, 1962, he was the first American to orbit the earth. In October of 1998 at age 77, he returned to the space program and traveled back into space. Neil Armstrong became the first man to walk on the moon. He was from Wapakoneta.
3. Ohio's state flag is a pennant design. It is the only state flag of that design in the United States.
4. The Glacial Grooves on the north side of Kelleys Island are the largest easily accessible such grooves in the world. They were scoured into solid limestone bedrock about 18,000 years ago by the great ice sheet that covered part of North America.
5. Thomas A. Edison from Milan developed the incandescent light bulb, phonograph, and early motion picture camera.
6. Long jumper DeHart Hubbard was the first African American to earn an Olympic Gold Medal. The award occurred during the 1924 Olympics games held in Paris. He set the record for long jumping. Jesse Owens grew up in Cleveland. He won four gold medals in the 1936 Olympics in Berlin.

OKLAHOMA

OKLAHOMA

Nickname: **THE SOONER STATE**

FLAG

CAR LICENSE PLATE

Redbud
Fabaceae Cercis Canadensis

Scissor-tailed Flycatcher
Tyrannus forficatus.

Mistletoe
Phoradendron serotinum

CAPITAL CITY	OKLAHOMA CITY
POPULATION	3,450,654 27TH LARGEST
ENTERED STATEHOOD	NOVEMBER 16, 1907, 46TH STATE
AREA	68679 sq.mi 20th Land 1224 sq.mi. 19th Water
BORDER STATE	Arkansas, Colorado, Kansas, Missouri, New Mexico, Texas ,
HIGHEST POINT	Black Mesa 4,973 ft. 23rd
LOWEST POINT	Little River; 287 feet, 34th
TOPOGRAPHY	High plains predominate in the west, hills and small mountains in the east; the east central region is dominated by the Arkansas River Basin and the Red River Plains are in the south.
ECONOMY	
AGRICULTURE	Cattle, wheat, milk, poultry, cotton
INDUSTRY	Transportation equipment, machinery, electric products, rubber and plastic products, food processing.

FAMOUS OKLAHOMANS

Johnny Bench	baseball player,
Jim Thorpe	athlete
Mickey Mantle	baseball player
Shannon Miller	Olympic gymnast
John Berryman	poet,
Tony Hillerman	author
Garth Brooks	singer
Reba McEntire	singer
Patti Page	singer
Vince Gill	singer
Woody Guthrie	singer, composer
Ike, Taylor, Zac Hanson	music
James Garner	actor
Brad Pitt	actor
Tony Randall	actor
Will Rogers	humorist
Maria Tallchief	ballerina
iron Eyes Cody	Cherokee
Wilma Mankiller	Cherokee chief
Owen K. Garriott	astronaut,
Gordon Cooper	astronaut
Shannon Lucid	astronaut
Oral Roberts	evangelist

- Tahlequah, Oklahoma is the Tribal capital of the Cherokee Nation.
- Spiro Mounds, Oklahoma's only archaeological park, is a 140-acre site encompassing 12 southern mounds that contain evidence of an Indian culture that occupied the site from 850 A.D. to 1450 A.D. The Mounds are considered one of the four most important prehistoric Indian sites east of the Rocky Mountains.
- Belle Starr one of the most famous women outlaws is buried in an isolated grave southwest of Porum, Oklahoma near the Eufuala Dam.
- Oklahoma has more man-made lakes than any other state, with over one million surface acres of water.
- Oklahoma has the largest Native American population of any state in the U.S. Many of the 250,000 American Indians living in Oklahoma are descended from the 67 tribes who inhabited the Indian Territory. Oklahoma is tribal headquarters for 39 tribes...
- Vinita is the oldest incorporated town on Oklahoma Route 66 being established in 1871. Vinita was the first town in Oklahoma to enjoy electricity. Originally named Downingville. The town's name was later changed to Vinita, in honor of Vinnie Ream, the sculptress who created the life-size statue of Lincoln at the United States Capitol.

OREGON

OREGON

Nickname: **BEAVER STATE**

Western Meadow Lark
Sturnella neglecta

Oregon Grape
Berberis aquifolium

Douglas-fir Pinaceae
Pseudotsuga menziesii

CAPITAL CITY	SALEM
POPULATION	4,447,100 23RD LARGEST STATE
ENTERED STATEHOOD	FEBRUARY 14, 1859 33RD STATE
BORDER STATE	CALIFORNIA, IDAHO, NEVADA, WASHINGTON
HIGHEST POINT	MOUNT HOOD 11,239 FT. .
LOWEST POINT	PACIFIC COAST, SEAL LEVEL
TOPOGRAPHY	RUGGED COAST RANGE, FERTILE WILIAMETTE RIVER VALLEY TO EAST AND SOUTH, CASCADE MOUNTAIN RANGE OF VOLCANIC PEAKS EAST OF THE VALLEY, PLATEAU EAST OF CASCADES, IN REMAINING TWO-THIRDS OF THE STATE.
AREA	96,003 SQ. MILES – 9TH LARGEST STATE 2383 SQ. MILES – 10TH IN WATER SIZE 296 MILES OF COASTLINE – 19TH IN SIZE 1410 MILES OF SHORELINE, 8TH IN SIZE
ECONOMY	
AGRICULTURE	CATTLE, VEGETABLES, NURSERY STOCK, FRUITS AND NUTS, DAIRY PRODUCTS, WHEAT.
INDUSTRY	LUMBER AND WOOD PRODUCTS, TOURISM, FOOD PROCESSING, PAPER PRODUCTS, MACHINERY, SCIENTIFIC INSTRUMENTS

FAMOUS OREGONIANS

Cecil D. Andrus	secretary of the interior
James Beard	food expert
Raymond Carver	writer, poet
Homer Davenport	political cartoonist
Douglas Engelbart	inventor
Matt Groening	cartoonist
Mark Hatfield	senator
Joni Huntley	track athlete
David Kennerly	photographer
Dave Kingman	baseball player
Edwin Markham	poet
inus Carl Pauling	chemist
Jane Powell	actress, singer
Steve Prefontaine	track athlete
John Reed	poet, journalist
Pat Schroeder	politician
Doc Severinsen	band leader
Sally Stanford	politician
Sally Struthers	actress,

- Oregon's state flag pictures a beaver on its reverse side. It is the only state flag to carry two separate designs.
- In 1880, a sea cave was discovered near what is now known as Florence. Sea Lion Caves is known to be the largest sea cave in the world.
- The Seaside Aquarium was the first facility in the world to successfully breed harbor seals in captivity.
- There are nine lighthouses standing along the coastline. Five are still being used; the others are designated historic monuments.
- High above the city of Portland the International Rose Test Garden features more than 500 varieties of roses cultivated continuously since 1917.
- Crater Lake is the deepest lake in the United States. It was formed more than 6,500 years ago, in the remains of an ancient volcano. Its crystal-blue waters are world-renowned.
- The Oregon Trail is the longest of the overland routes used in the westward expansion of the United States.
- Haystack Rock off Cannon Beach is 235 feet high and is the third largest coastal monolith in the world.
- The Tillamook Rock Lighthouse, built in 1880, is currently used as the site of the final resting place of up to 467,000 cremated individuals.

PENNSYLVANIA

PENNSYLVANIA

Nickname: **THE KEYSTONE STATE**

FLAG

CAR LICENSE PLATE

Ruffed Grouse
TETRAO UMBELLUS

Mountain Laurel
Kalmia latiflolia

Eastern hemlock
Pinaceae Tsuga Canadensi

FAMOUS PENNSYLVANIANS

James Buchanan	U.S. President
Louisa May Alcott	author
John Updike	author
John Barrymore	actor
Bill Cosby	actor
Gene Kelly	dancer, actor
Tom Mix	actor
James Stewart	actor
Mary Cassatt	painter
Andrew Wyeth	painter
Alexander Calder	sculptor
Daniel Boone	frontiersman
Jimmy Dorsey	band leader
Tommy Dorsey	band leader
Stephen Foster	composer
W. C. Fields	comedian
Robert Fulton	inventor
Lee Iacocca	auto executive
Reggie Jackson	baseball player
Tara Lipinski	figure skater
Margaret Mead	anthropologist
Arnold Palmer	golfer

CAPITAL CITY	HARRISBURG
POPULATION	12, 281,054 6TH LARGEST STATE
ENTERED STATEHOOD	DECEMBER 12, 1787, 2ND STATE
BORDER STATE	DELAWARE, MARYLAND, NEW JERSEY, NEW YORK, OHIO, WEST VIRGINIA
HIGHEST POINT	MT. DAVIS, 3213 FEET
LOWEST POINT	DELAWARE RIVER, SEAL LEVEL
TOPOGRAPHY	ALLEGHENY MOUNTAINS RUN SOUTHWEST TO NORTHEAST, WITH PIEDMONT AND COASTAL PLAIN IN SOUTHEAST TRIANGLE. ALLEGHENY FRONT A DIAGONAL SPINE ACROSS THE STATES CENTER, NORTHWEST RUGGED PLATEAU FALLS TO LAKE ERIE LOWLANDS.
AREA	44820 SQUARE MILES – 33RD LAND SIZE 1239 SQUARE MILES – 32ND WATER SIZE 53 MILES OF COASTLINE – 17TH IN SIZE 607 MILES SHORELINE – 19TH IN SIZE
ECONOMY	
AGRICULTURE	DAIRY PRODUCTS, POULTRY, CATTLE, NURSERY STOCK, MUSHROOMS, HOGS, HAY
INDUSTRY	FOOD PROCESSING, CHEMICAL PRODUCTS, MACHINERY, ELECTRIC EQUIPMENT, TOURISM

- In 1913, the first automobile service station opened in Pittsburgh.
- The first daily newspaper was published in Philadelphia on Sept. 21, 1784.
- Drake Well Museum in Titusville is on the site where Edwin L. Drake drilled the world's first oil well in 1859 and launched the modern petroleum industry.
- Philadelphia is the site of the first presidential mansion.
- Betsy Ross made the first American flag in Philadelphia.
- "Doctor, if you don't give me something to help me breathe, I'm going to stop!" came the urgent cry of 16-year old Frederick Gable of Loganville. Vowing not to lose another patient to pneumonia, Dr. George Holtzapple successfully created the first application of oxygen, thus saving his patient's life and winning international fame through his discovery. The year was 1885.
- The Declaration of Independence was signed in Philadelphia in 1776 and is home to the Liberty Bell.
- Fairmount Park in Philadelphia is the largest city park with over 8,000 acres.

RHODE ISLAND

RHODE ISLAND

Nickname: **THE OCEAN STATE**

CAR LICENSE PLATE

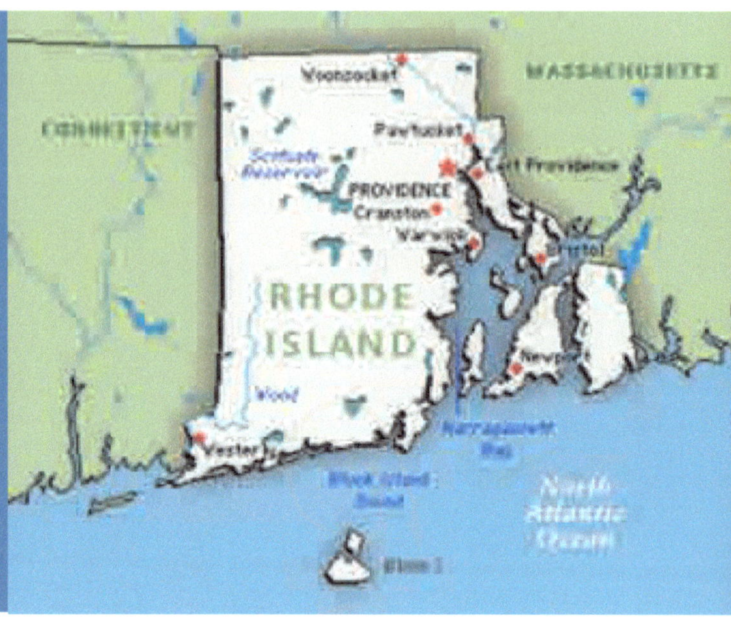

Rhode Island Red

Common Blue Violet
Viola sororia

Red maple
Aceraceae Acer rubrum

FAMOUS RHODE LSLANDERS

George M Cohan	Song/music writer
Roger Williams	Politician
Nelson Eddy	Singer, actor
Jabez Gorham	Silversmith
David Hartman	TV newscaster
Ida Lewis	Lighthouse keeper
Matthew Perry	Navel Officer
Oliver Perry	Navel Officer
Gilbert Stuart	Painter

CAPITAL CITY	PROVIDENCE
POPULATION	4,447,100 23RD LARGEST STATE
ENTERED STATEHOOD	MAY 29, 1790, 13TH STATE
BORDER STATE	CONNECTICUT, MASSACHUSETTS, NEW YORK
HIGHEST POINT	JERIMOTH HILL, 812 FT.
LOWEST POINT	ATLANTIC COAST/ OCEAN, SEA LEVEL
TOPOGRAPHY	EASTERN LOWLANDS OF NARRAGANSETT BASIN, WESTERN UPLANDS OF FLAT ROLLING HILLS
AREA	1045 SQUARE MILES – 50TH LAND SIZE 500 SQUARE MILES – 50TH WATER SIZE 40 MILES OF COASTLINE – 41ST IN SIZE 384 MILES SHORELINE – 19TH IN SIZE
ECONOMY	
AGRICULTURE	NURSERY STOCK, VEGETABLES, DAIRY PRODUCTS, EGGS
INDUSTRY	FASHION JEWELRY, FABRICATED METAL PRODUCTS, ELECTRIC EQUIPMENT, SHIPBUILDING/ BOATBUILDING, MACHINERY, TOURISM

- Rhode Island is the smallest state in size in the United States. It covers an area of 1,214 square miles. Its distances North to South are 48 miles and East to West 37 miles.
- The Cogswell Tower in Central Falls was the site of an Indian observation point in use during King Phillips War in 1676. The tower was built in 1904 as part of the last will and testament of Caroline Cogswell.
- Polo was played for the first time in the United States in 1876 near Newport.
- St. Mary's, Rhode Island's oldest Roman Catholic parish was founded in 1828. The church is best known as the site of the wedding of Jacqueline Bouvier to John Fitzgerald Kennedy in 1953.
- The Flying Horse Carousel is the nation's oldest carousel. It is located in the resort town of Watch Hill.
- At the Point Judith corrosion test site material samples sit exposed for years and are analyzed to determine the toll taken by ocean air and the sun.
- Rhode Islanders were the first to take military action against England by sinking one of her ships in the Narragansett Bay located between Newport and Providence. The English ship was called "The Gaspee".
- Thomas Jefferson and John Adams publicly acknowledged Roger Williams, as the originator of the concepts and principles reflected in The First Amendment. Among those principles were freedom of religion, freedom of speech, and freedom of public assembly.
- The era known The Industrial Revolution started in Rhode Island with the development and construction in 1790 of Samuel Slater's water-powered cotton mill in Pawtucket.
- At Little Compton is home to the gravesite of the first girl born to colonists in New England. The baby was the daughter of pilgrims John and Priscilla Alden.
- Built in 1880 Channing Memorial Church was named for William Ellery Channing, a leader in the Unitarian Church and the abolitionist movement. Julia Ward Howe, author of the "Battle Hymn of the Republic", attended this church.
- New England's oldest Masonic Temple in Warren was built in the 18th century with timbers from British frigates sunk in Newport Harbor during the Revolutionary War.
- The Touro Synagogue is the oldest synagogue in North America. Built in 1763 the synagogue houses the oldest torah in North America.

SOUTH CAROLINA

SOUTH CAROLINA

Nickname:
THE PALMETTO STATE

FLAG

CAR LICENSE PLATE

Carolina wren
Thryothorus ludovicianus

Yellow Jessamine
Gelsemium sempervirens

Cabbage palmetto
Arecaceae Sabal palmetto

FAMOUS SOUTH CAROLINIANS

Andrew Jackson	U.S. President
Jesse L. Jackson	Civil Rights Leader
William Westmorland	Army Chief of Staff
Strom Thurmond	Politician
Francis Marion	General
Ertha Kitt	Singer
Althea Gibson	Tennis Champion

CAPITAL CITY	COLUMBIA
POPULATION	4,012,012 26TH LARGEST STATE
ENTERED STATEHOOD	MAY 23, 1788, 8TH STATE
BORDER STATE	GEORGIA, NORTH CAROLINA
HIGHEST POINT	SASSAFRAS MOUNTAIN, 3,500 FT
LOWEST POINT	ATLANTIC COAST, SEA LEVEL
TOPOGRAPHY	BLUE RIDGE PROVINCE IN NORTHWEST HAS HIGHEST PEAKS, PIEDMONT LIES BETWEEN THE MOUNTAINS AND FALL LINE, COASTAL PLAIN COVERS TWO-THIRDS OF THE STATE
AREA	30,111 SQUARE MILES – 40TH LAND SIZE 1896 SQUARE MILES – 40TH WATER SIZE 187 MILES OF COASTLINE – 21ST IN SIZE 2,876 MILES OF SHORELINE – 11TH IN SIZE
ECONOMY	
AGRICULTURE	TOBACCO, POULTRY, CATTLE, DAIRY PRODUCTS, SOYBEANS, HOGS
INDUSTRY	TEXTILE GOODS, CHEMICAL PRODUCTS, PAPER PRODUCTS, MACHINERY, TOURISM, APPAREL, TRANSPORTATION EQUIPMENT

- The walls of the American fort on Sullivan Island, in Charleston Harbor, were made of spongy Palmetto logs. This was helpful in protecting the fort because the British cannonballs bounced off the logs.
- The first battle of the Civil War took place at Fort Sumter.
- The Black River Swamp Preserve is located near Andrews. This slow-moving river is characterized by high concentrations of organic carbon, which accounts for the tea-colored water and gives rise to the diverse habitats in its widespread floodplain.
- Every few years, Irmo has a sighting of some kind of water monster that inhabits Lake Murray. The monster first 'surfaced' in 1973 when residents of Irmo and Ballentine saw a cousin of the Loch Ness Monster. It was described in The Independent News in 1980 as "a cross between a snake and something prehistoric."
- Sweetgrass basket making has been a part of the Mount Pleasant community for more than 300 years. Basket making is a traditional art form that has been passed on from generation to generation.
- Bomb Island on Lake Murray each spring and summer is the home of a very unusual event. Each year thousands of Purple Martins return to this island to roost for the summer. The island has been declared a bird sanctuary and it is quite a sight to watch these birds return to Bomb Island each day around sunset

SOUTH DAKOTA

SOUTH DAKOTA

Nickname:
THE MOUNT RUSHMORE STATE

FLAG

CAR LICENSE PLATE

White spruce
Pinaceae Picea glauca

Ring-necked Pheasant

Pasque Flower
Ppulsatilla hirsutissima

FAMOUS SOUTH DAKOTANS

Tom Brokaw	TV newscaster
Crazy Horse	Oglala chief
Oscar Howe	Sioux artist
Hubert.H. Humphrey	Senator & Vice-President
Cheryl Ladd	Actress
Dorothy Provine	Actress
Rain-in-the-Face	Hunkpapa Sioux chief
Red Cloud	Oglala Sioux chief
Sitting Bull	Hunkpappa Sioux chief

CAPITAL CITY	PIERRE
POPULATION	754,844 46TH LARGEST STATE
ENTERED STATEHOOD	NOVEMBER 2, 1889, 40TH STATE
BORDER STATE	IOWA, MINNESOTA, MONTANA, NEBRASKA, NORTH DAKOTA, WYOMING
HIGHEST POINT	HARNEY PEAK, 7242 FEET
LOWEST POINT	BIG STONE LAKE, 962 FEET
TOPOGRAPHY	PRARIE PLAINS IN THE EAST, ROLLING HILLS OF THE GREAT PLAINS IN THE WEST, BLACK HILLS IN THE SOUTHWEST CORNER
AREA	75,898 SQUARE MILES – 17TH LAND SIZE 1224 SQUARE MILES – 16TH WATER SIZE
ECONOMY	
AGRICULTURE	CATTLE, HOGS, WHEAT, SOYBEANS, MILK, CORN
INDUSTRY	FOOD PROCESSING, MACHINERY, LUMBER AND WOOD PRODUCTS, TOURISM

- Sculptor Gutzon Borglum began drilling into the 6,200-foot Mount Rushmore in 1927. Creation of the Shrine to Democracy took 14 years and cost a mere $1 million, though it is now deemed priceless. The faces of George Washington, Thomas Jefferson, Theodore Roosevelt, and Abraham Lincoln are sculpted into Mount Rushmore the world's greatest mountain carving.
- The site of a rich gold strike in 1875, Deadwood retains its mining town atmosphere. While Deadwood is one of the most highly publicized mining towns of the trans-Mississippi West, much of its fame rests on the famous or infamous characters that passed through.
- Belle Fourche is the geographical center of the United States of America, designated in 1959 and noted by an official marker and sheepherder's monument called a "Stone Johnnie".
- South Dakota is the home of the Dakota, Lakota and Nakota tribes, which make up the Sioux Nation.
- Custer State Park is home to a herd of 1,500 free-roaming bison. Bison can weigh as much as 2,000 pounds. Historically, the bison played an essential role in the lives of the Lakota (Sioux), who relied on the "tatanka" for food, clothing and shelter.
- The Mammoth Site of Hot Springs contains the largest concentration of Columbian and woolly mammoth bones discovered in their primary context in the world! This National Natural Landmark is the only in-situ (bones left as found) display of fossil mammoths in America.
- The Flaming Fountain on South Dakota State Capitol Lake is fed by an artesian well with natural gas content so high that it can be lit. The fountain glows perpetually as a memorial to all veterans.

TENNESSEE

TENNESSEE

Nickname: **THE VOLUNTEER STATE**

FLAG

CAR LICENSE PLATE

Yellow poplar
Magnoliaceae Liriodendron tulipifera

Mockingbird
Mimus polyglottos

Iris
Iridaceae

FAMOUS TENNESEANS

Andrew Johnson	U.S. President
Polly Bergen	Actress-Singer
Hattie Caraway	1st Elected Woman Senator
Davey Crockett	Frontiersman
Dolly Parton	Singer
Sequoia	Cherokee Scholar, educator
Carl Rowan	Journalist

CAPITAL CITY	Nashville
POPULATION	5, 689,283 16TH Largest State
ENTERED STATEHOOD	June 1, 1796, 16TH State
BORDER STATE	Alabama, Arkansas, Georgia, Kentucky, Mississippi, Missouri, North Carolina, Virginia
HIGHEST POINT	Clingman's Dome, 6,643 FT.
LOWEST POINT	Mississippi River, 182 FT.
TOPOGRAPHY	Rugged country in the east, Great Smokey Mountains, low ridges in the Appalachian valley, the flat Cumberland plateau, slightly rolling terrain and knobs of the interior low plateau, the largest region, eastern gulf coastal plain to the west, laced with meandering streams. Mississippi Alluvial Plain, a narrow strip of swamp and flood plain in the extreme west.
AREA	41,220 SQ. miles – 36TH Land size 926 SQ. miles – 34TH water size
ECONOMY	
AGRICULTURE	Soybeans, cotton, tobacco, livestock and livestock products, dairy products, cattle, hogs.
INDUSTRY	Chemicals, transportation equipment, rubber, plastics.

- Iroquois, bred at Nashville's Belle Meade Plantation, was the first American winner of the English Derby in 1881. Such modern thoroughbreds as Secretariat trace their bloodlines to Iroquois.
- The Copper Basin is so different from the surrounding area it has been seen and is recognizable by American astronauts.
- Nashville's Grand Ole Opry is the longest continuously running live radio program in the world. It has broadcast every Friday and Saturday night since 1925.
- The legendary railroad engineer Casey Jones, who was killed when his train crashed on April 30, 1900, lived in Jackson.
- Elvis Presley's home called Graceland is located in Memphis. Graceland is the second most visited house in the country.
- The National Civil Rights Museum in Memphis is at the Lorraine Motel where Dr. Martin Luther King, Jr. was slain in 1968. The museum preserves the motel and tells the history of the American Civil Rights Movement.
- The "Guinness Book of World Records" lists the Lost Sea in Sweetwater as the largest underground lake in the United States.
- The Cherokee silversmith, Sequoyah, was the only known man in the history of the world to single-handedly develop an alphabet. His syllabus for the Cherokee Nation resulted in the first written language for a Native American people.
- The world's largest artificial skiing surface is located at the Ober Gatlinburg Ski Resort in Gatlinburg. There a 5-acre artificial ski surface permits skiing in any type of weather.
- Coca-Cola was first bottled in 1899 at a plant on Patten Parkway in downtown Chattanooga after two local attorneys purchased the bottling rights to the drink for $l.00.
- Cotton made Memphis a major port on the Mississippi River. The Memphis Cotton Exchange still handles approximately one-third of the entire American cotton crop each year.

TEXAS

Nickname: ***THE LONE STAR STATE***

FLAG

CAR LICENSE PLATE

Pecan
Juglandaceae Carya illinoinensis (illinoensis)

Mockingbird
Mimus polyglottos

Bluebonnet
Lupinus

FAMOUS TEXANS

DWIGHT D. EISENHOWER	U.S. PRESIDENT
LYNDON B. JOHNSON	U.S. PRESIDENT
RED ADAIR	OIL WELL FIREMAN
MARY KAY ASH	COSMETICS ENTREPENEUR
GENE AUTRY	SINGER, TV COWBOY
CLYDE BARROW	OUTLAW
BONNIE PARKER	OUTLAW
CAROL BURNETT	COMEDIENNE
DENTON COOLEY	HEART SURGEON
A.J. FOYT	AUTO RACER
BEN HOGAN	GOLFER
BUDDY HOLLY	MUSICIAN
AUDIE MURPHY	WAR HERO, ACTOR
SANDRA DAY O'CONNER	SUPREME COURT JUSTICE
BABE DIDRIKSON ZAHARIAS	GOLFER, ATHLETE

CAPITAL CITY	AUSTIN
POPULATION	20,851,820 2ND LARGEST STATE
ENTERED STATEHOOD	DECEMBER 29, 1845 28TH STATE
BORDER STATE	ARKANSAS, LOUISIANA, NEW MEXICO, OKLAHOMA
HIGHEST POINT	GUADALUPE PEAK, 8,749 FT.
LOWEST POINT	GULF COAST, SEA LEVEL
TOPOGRAPHY	GULF COAST PLAIN IN THE SOUTH AND SOUTH-EAST, NORTH CENTRAL PLAINS SLOPE UPWARD WITH SOME HILLS, GREAT PLAINS EXTEND OVER THE PANHANDLE, ARE BROKEN BY LOW MOUNTAINS, TRANS-PECOS ARE SOUTHERN EXTENSION OF THE ROCKY MOUNTAINS
AREA	261914 SQUARE MILES – 2ND LAND SIZE 6687 SQUARE MILES – 2ND WATER SIZE
ECONOMY	
AGRICULTURE	CATTLE, COTTON, DAIRY PRODUCTS, NURSERY STOCK, POULTRY, SORGHUM, CORN, WHEAT
INDUSTRY	CHEMICAL PRODUCTS, PETROLEUM AND NATURAL GAS, FOOD PROCESSING, ELECTRIC EQUIPMENT, MACHINERY, MINING, TOURISM

- The Alamo is located in San Antonio. It is where Texas defenders fell to Mexican General Santa Anna and the phrase Remember the Alamo originated.
- The King Ranch in Texas is bigger than the state of Rhode Island.
- During the period of July 24-26, 1979, the Tropical Storm Claudette brought 45 inches of rain to an area near Alvin, Texas, contributing to more than $600 million in damages. Claudette produced the United States 24 hour rainfall record of 43 inches.
- More wool comes from the state of Texas than any other state in the United States.
- Edwards Plateau in west central Texas is the top sheep growing area in the country.
- Texas boasts the nation's largest herd of whitetail deer.
- A coastal live oak located near Fulton is the oldest tree in the state. The tree has an estimated age of more than 1,500 years.
- Caddo Lake is the only natural lake in the state.
- The first suspension bridge in the United States was the Waco Bridge. Built in 1870 and still in use today as a pedestrian crossing of the Brazos River.
- The first word spoken from the moon on July 20, 1969 was Houston.

UTAH

UTAH

Nickname: **THE BEEHIVE STATE**

FLAG

CAR LICENSE PLATE

California Gull
Larus californicus

Sego lily
Calochortus gunnisonii

Blue spruce
Pinaceae Picea pungens

FAMOUS UTAHNS

Butch Cassidy	Western Outlaw
Philo T. Farnswoth	Inventor of Television
Maude Adams	Chess Champion
Frank Borzage	Film director, producer
John M. Browning	inventor
Avard Fairbanks	sculptor
Howard A. Jarvis	social reformer
J. Willard Marriott	restaurant, hotel chain founder
Peter Skene Ogden	fur trader
Donny Osmond,	singer
Marie Osmond	singer
Virginia Sorensen	author
Mack Swain	actor
Everett Thorpe	painter
Robert Walker	actor
Marie Windsor	actress
James Woods	actor

CAPITAL CITY	SALT LAKE CITY
POPULATION	2,233,169 34TH LARGEST STATE
ENTERED STATEHOOD	JANUARY 4, 1896 45TH STATE
BORDER STATES	ARIZONA, COLORADO, IDAHO, NEVADA, NEW MEXICO, WYOMING
HIGHEST POINT	KINGS PEAK, 13,528 FT.
LOWEST POINT	BEAVERDAM CREAK, 2000 FT.
TOPOGRAPHY	HIGH COLORADO PLATEAU CUT BY BRILLIANTLY COLORED CANYONS IN THE SOUTHEAST, BROADER FLAT, DESERT LIKE GREAT B ASIN OF THE WEST, THE GREAT SALT LAKE AND BONNEVILLE SALT FLATS IN THE NORTHWEST, MIDDLE ROCKIES IN THE NORTHWEST RUNNING EAST-WEST, VALLEYS AND PLATEAUS OF THE WASATCH FRONT.
AREA	82,168 SQUARE MILES – 13TH LAND SIZE 2736 SQUARE MILES – 12TH WATER SIZE
ECONOMY	
AGRICULTURE	CATTLE, DAIRY PRODUCTS, HAY, TURKEYS
INDUSTRY	MACHINERY, AEROSPACE, MINING, FOOD PROCESSING, ELECTRIC EQUIPMENT, TOURISM

- Completion of the world's first transcontinental railroad was celebrated at Promontory where the Central Pacific and Union Pacific Railroads met on May 10, 1869. It is now known as Golden Spike National Historic Site
- Utah is the site of the nation's first department store. Zions Co-operative Mercantile Institution was established in the late 1800's. It is still in operation today as ZCMI.
- The Mormon Temple in Salt Lake City took 40 years to complete.
- Rainbow Bridge, Nature's abstract sculpture carved of solid sandstone, is the world's largest natural-rock span. It stands 278 feet wide and 309 feet high.
- The Great Salt Lake covers 2,100 square miles, with an average depth of 13 feet. The deepest point is 34 feet.
- The average snowfall in the mountains near Salt Lake City is 500 inches. Because of the state's inland location, Utah's snow is unusually dry, earning it the reputation of having the world's greatest powder. Annual precipitation varies from less than five inches in Utah's arid Great Salt Lake Desert to more than 60 inches in the northern mountain ranges.
- Utah has 11,000 miles of fishing streams and 147,000 acres of lakes and reservoirs.
- Utah has the highest literacy rate in the nation.
- Capitol Reef National Park protects The Waterpocket Fold a 100-mile long wrinkle in the earth's crust known to geologists as a monocline. The Waterpocket Fold extends from Thousand Lakes Mountain to the Colorado River.

VERMONT

Nickname: ***THE GREEN MOUNTAIN STATE***

FLAG

CAR LICENSE PLATE

Sugar maple
Aceraceae
Acer saccharum

HERMIT THRUSH.
TURDUS SOLITARIUS

Red Clover
Trifolium pretense

FAMOUS VERMONTERS

CHESTER A. ARTHUR	U.S. PRESIDENT
CALVIN COOLIDGE	U.S. PRESIDENT

CAPITAL CITY	MONTPELIER
POPULATION	608,827 49TH LARGEST STATE
ENTERED STATEHOOD	MARCH 4, 1791 14TH STATE
BORDER STATES	MASSACHUSETTS, NEW HAMPSHIRE, NEW YORK
HIGHEST POINT	MT. MANSFIELD, 4,393 FT.
LOWEST POINT	LAKE CHAMPLAIN, 95 FT.
TOPOGRAPHY	GREEN MOUNTAINS CREATE NORTH-SOUTH BACKBONE 20-30 MILES WIDE, AVERAGE ALTITUDE APPROXIMATELY 1,000 FT.TERRAIN
AREA	9249 SQUARE MILES – 45TH LAND SIZE 306 SQUARE MILES – 43RD WATER SIZE
ECONOMY	
AGRICULTURE	DAIRY PRODUCTS, CATTLE, HAY, APPLES, MAPLE PRODUCTS
INDUSTRY	ELECTRONIC EQUIPMENT, FABRICATED METAL PRODUCTS, PRINTING AND PUBLISHING, PAPER PRODUCTS, TOURISM

- Montpelier, Vermont is the only U.S. state capital without a McDonalds.
- Montpelier, Is the largest producer of maple syrup in the U.S.
- Ben & Jerry's Ice Cream company gives their ice cream waste to the local Vermont farmers who use it to feed their hogs. The hogs seem to like all of the flavors except Mint Oreo.
- Rudyard Kipling, living in Vermont in the 1890's invented the game of snow golf.
- Vermont does not sell alcohol to out of state licenses, you must have a liquor ID in order to purchase alcohol at liquor stores and grocery stores.

VIRGINIA

VIRGINIA

Nickname: ***THE OLD DOMINION***

FLAG

CAR LICENSE PLATE

Flowering dogwood
Cornaceae Cornus florida

Cardinal
(Cardinalis cardinalis)

American Dogwood
Cornus florida

FAMOUS VIRGINIANS

GEORGE WASHINGTON	U.S. PRESIDENT
THOMAS JEFFERSON	U.S. PRESIDENT
JAMES MADISON	U.S. PRESIDENT
JAMES MONROE	U.S. PRESIDENT
WILLIAM H. HARRISON	U.S. PRESIDENT
JOHN TYLER	U.S. PRESIDENT
ZACHARY TAYLOR	U.S. PRESIDENT
WOODROW WILSON	U.S. PRESIDENT

CAPITAL CITY	RICHMOND
POPULATION	7,078,515 12TH LARGEST STATE
ENTERED STATEHOOD	UNE 25, 1788, 10TH STATE
BORDER STATES	KENTUCKY, MARYLAND, NORTH CARO-INA, TENNESSEE, WEST VIRGINIA
HIGHEST POINT	MT. ROGERS, 5,729 FT.
LOWEST POINT	ATLANTIC COAST, SEA LEVEL
TOPOGRAPHY	MOUNTAIN AND VALLEY REGION IN THE WEST, INCLUDING THE BLUE RIDGE MOUNTAINS, ROLLING PIEDMONT PLATEAU, TIDEWATER OR COASTAL PLAIN, INCLUDING THE EASTERN SHORE.
AREA	39,598 SQUARE MILES – 35TH LAND SIZE 3171 SQUARE MILES – 37TH WATER SIZE 112 MILES OF COASTLINE – 13TH IN SIZE 3,315 MILES OF SHORELINE – 15TH IN SIZE
ECONOMY	
AGRICULTURE	CATTLE, POULTRY, DAIRY PRODUCTS, TOBACCO, HOGS, SOYBEANS
INDUSTRY	TRANSPORTATION EQUIPMENT, TEXTILES, FOOD PROCESSING, PRINTING, ELECTRIC EQUIPMENT, CHEMICALS

- Virginia was named for England's "Virgin Queen," Elizabeth I.
- The College of William and Mary in Williamsburg is the second oldest in the United States, it was founded in 1693.
- The State flower is not really a flower, but the blossom of the dogwood tree, which is the state tree.
- About 1/2 of all the people in the United States live within a 500 mile radius of the Capital of Virginia.
- In Virginia, more people work for the United States government than any other industry. About 1/4 of Virginia's workers.
- Virginia's largest private employer is also the world's largest ship building yard.
- Wild Ponies have roamed freely on Assateague Island for centuries.
- Bristol is legally two cities but they share the same main street. One in Virginia and one in Tennessee each with its own government and city services.

WASHINGTON

Nickname: **THE EVERGREEN STATE**

FLAG

CAR LICENSE PLATE

WILLOW GOLDFINCH
[Carduelis tristis.]

Coast Rhododendron
Rhododendron macrophvllum

Western Hemlock
Pinaceae Tsuga heterophylla

FAMOUS WASHINGTONIANS

Howard Duff	actor	**Dyan Cannon**	actress
John McIntire	actor	**Frances Farmer**	actress
Adam West	actor	**Carol Channing**	actress
Kurt Cobain	grunge rock icon	**Bing Crosby**	singer, actor
Jimmie Rogers	singe	**Judy Collins**	singer
Bob Crosby	musician	**Patrice Munsel**	soprano
Merce Cunningham	choreographer	**Kenny Loggins**	singer, songwriter
Jimi Hendrix	Guitarist	**Chester F. Carlson**	inventor
Robert Joffrey	choreographer	**Bill Gates**	Software Executive
John Walker Kendall	Scientist	**Francis Scobee**	astronaut
Seattle Dwamish	Suquamish chief	**Smohalla**	Indian prophet & chief

CAPITAL CITY	OLYMPIA
POPULATION	5,894,121 15TH LARGEST STATE
ENTERED STATEHOOD	NOVEMBER 11, 1889 42ND STATE
BORDER STATE	IDAHO, OREGON (NORTHERN BORDER-CANADA) MISSISSIPPI, TENNESSEE
HIGHEST POINT	MT. RAINIER, 14,410 FT.
LOWEST POINT	PACIFIC COAST, SEA LEVEL
TOPOGRAPHY	OLYMPIC MOUNTAINS ON THE NORTHWEST PENNINSULA, OPEN LAND ALONG COAST TO COLUMBIA RIVER, FLAT TERRAIN OF PUGET SOUND LOWLAND, CASCADE MOUNTAINS HIGH PEAKS TO THE EAST OF LOWLAND, COLUMBIA BASIN IN CENTRAL PORTION, HIGHLANDS TO THE NORTHEAST, MOUNTAINS TO THE SOUTHEAST
AREA	66,582 SQUARE MILES – 18th LAND SIZE 4721 SQUARE MILES – 20th WATER SIZE 157 MILES OF COASTLINE – 11TH IN SIZE 3,026 MILES OF SHORELINE – 12TH IN SIZE
ECONOMY	
AGRICULTURE	SEAFOOD, DAIRY PRODUCTS, APPLES, CATTLE, WHEAT, POTATOES, NURSERY STOCK
INDUSTRY	AEROSPACE, SOFTWARE DEVELOPMENT, FOOD PROCESSING, PAPER PRODUCTS, LUMBER AND WOOD PRODUCTS, CHEMICAL PRODUCTS, TOURISM

- The state of Washington is the only state to be named after a United States president.
- Washington state produces more apples than any other state in the union.
- Washington state has more glaciers than the other 47 contiguous states combined.
- Everett is the site of the world's largest building, Boeing's final assembly plant
- The Governor Albert D. Rosellini Bridge at Evergreen Point is the longest floating bridge in the world. The bridge connects Seattle and Medina across Lake Washington.
- Puget Sound's many islands are served by the largest ferry fleet in the United States.
- In 1980, the northeast face of Mount St. Helens exploded outward, destroying a large part of the top of the volcano.
- The percentage of non-religious people in Washington is the highest of any state, and church membership is among the lowest of all states.

WEST VIRGINIA

Nickname: **THE MOUNTAIN STATE**

FLAG

CAR LICENSE PLATE

Sugar maple
Aceraceae Acer saccharum

Cardinal
(Cardinalis cardinalis)

Rhododendron
Rhododendron maximum

FAMOUS WEST VIRGINIANS

Pearl Buck	Author
Peter Marshall	Television Host
Chuck Yeager	Test Pilot-Air Force General
Don Knotts	Actor
Mary Lou Retton	Olympic Gold Medalist-Gymnastics
Kathy Mattea	Country Music Singer.

CAPITAL CITY	CHARLESTON
POPULATION	1,808,344 37TH LARGEST STATE
ENTERED STATEHOOD	JUNE 20, 1863 35TH STATE
BORDER STATEK	KENTUCKY, MARYLAND,OHIO, PENNSYLVANIA, VIRGINIA
HIGHEST POINT	SPRUCE KNOB 4,863 FT.
LOWEST POINT	POTOMAC RIVER 240 FT.
TOPOGRAPHY	RANGING FROM HILLY TO MOUNTAINOUS, ALLEHENY PLATEAU, IN THE WEST, COVERS TWO-THIRDS OF THE STATE, MOUNTAINS OVER 4,000 FEET.
AREA	24,087 SQUARE MILES – 41ST LAND SIZE 145 SQUARE MILES – 50TH WATER SIZE
ECONOMY	
AGRICULTURE	CATTLE, DAIRY PRODUCTS, POULTRY, APPLES
INDUSTRY	CHEMICAL PRODUCTS, MINING, PRIMARY METALS, STONE, CLAY AND GLASS PRODUCTS, TOURISM

- Mother's Day was first observed at Andrews Church in Grafton on May 10, 1908.
- The world's largest sycamore tree is located on the Back Fork of the Elk River in Webster Springs.
- On January 26, 1960 Danny Heater, a student from Burnsville, scored 135 points in a high school basketball game earning him a place in the Guinness Book of World Records.
- The first federal prison exclusively for women in the United States was opened in 1926 in West Virginia.
- The New River Gorge Bridge near Fayetteville is the second highest steel arch bridge in the United States. The bridge is also the longest steel arch bridge (1,700 feet) in the world. Every October on Bridge Day, the road is closed and individuals parachute and bungee cord jump 876 feet off the bridge. It's West Virginia's largest single day event and attracts about 100,000 people each year.
- One of the nation's oldest and largest Indian burial grounds is located in Moundsville. Its 69 feet high, 900 feet in circumference, and 50 feet high. An inscribed stone was removed from the vault and is on display at the Smithsonian Institute in Washington, D.C.
- Nearly 75% of West Virginia is covered by forests.
- 15% of the nation's total coal production comes from West Virginia.
- West Virginia's Memorial Tunnel was the first in the nation to be monitored by television. It opened November 8, 1954.
- Coal House, the only residence in the world built entirely of coal is located in White Sulphur Springs. The house was occupied on June 1, 1961.
- Stone that was quarried near Hinton was contributed by West Virginia for the Washington Monument
- Mrs. Minnie Buckingham Harper, a member of the House of Delegates by appointment in 1928, was the first African American woman to become a member of a legislative body in the United States.

WISCONSIN

WISCONSIN

Nickname:
THE BADGER STATE

FLAG

CAR LICENSE PLATE

Sugar maple
Aceraceae Acer saccharum

ROBIN
TURDUS
MIGRA TORIUS

Wood Violet
Viola papilionacea

FAMOUS WISCONSINITES

FRANK LLOYD WRIGHT	ARCHETECT
HARRY HOUDINI	MAGICIAN & ESCAPE ARTIST
DOUGLAS MACARTHUR	WWII & KOREAN WAR GENERAL
DON AMECHE	ACTOR
L.L. HINTZ	GUIDE

CAPITAL CITY	MADISON
POPULATION	5,363,675 18TH LARGEST STATE
ENTERED STATEHOOD	MAY 29, 1848 30TH STATE
BORDER STATE	ILLINOIS, IOWA, MICHIGAN, MINNESOTA
HIGHEST POINT	TIMMS HILL, 1,951 FT.
LOWEST POINT	SHORE OF LAKE MICHIGAN, 581 FT.
TOPOGRAPHY	NARROW LAKE SUPERIOR LOWLAND PLAIN MET BY NORTHERN HIGHLAND, WHICH SLOPES GENTLY TO THE SANDY CRESCENT CENTRAL PLAIN. WESTERN UPLAND IN THE SOUTHWEST, THREE BROAD PARALLEL LIMESTONE RIDGES RUNNING NORTH-SOUTH ARE SEPERATED BY WIDE AND SHALLOW LOWLAND IN THE SOUTHEAST.
AREA	54,314 SQUARE MILES – 23RD LAND SIZE 11,190 SQUARE MILES – 25TH WATER SIZE
ECONOMY	
AGRICULTURE	CHEESE, DAIRY PRODUCTS, CATTLE, HOGS, VEGETABLES, CORN, CRANBERRIES
INDUSTRY	MACHINERY, FOOD PROCESSING, PAPER PRODUCTS, ELECTRIC EQUIPMENT, FABRICATED METAL METAL PRODUCTS, TOURISM

- Wisconsin visitors and residents enjoy the state's 7,446 streams and rivers. End-to-end they'd stretch 26,767 miles. That is more than enough to circle the globe at the equator.
- The House on the Rock was designed and built in the early 1940s. It is considered an architectural marvel and is perched on a 60-foot chimney of rock. The 14-room house is now a complex of rooms, streets, buildings, and gardens covering over 200 acres. The Infinity Room contains 3,264 windows.

WYOMING

WYOMING

Nickname: **THE EQUALITY STATE**

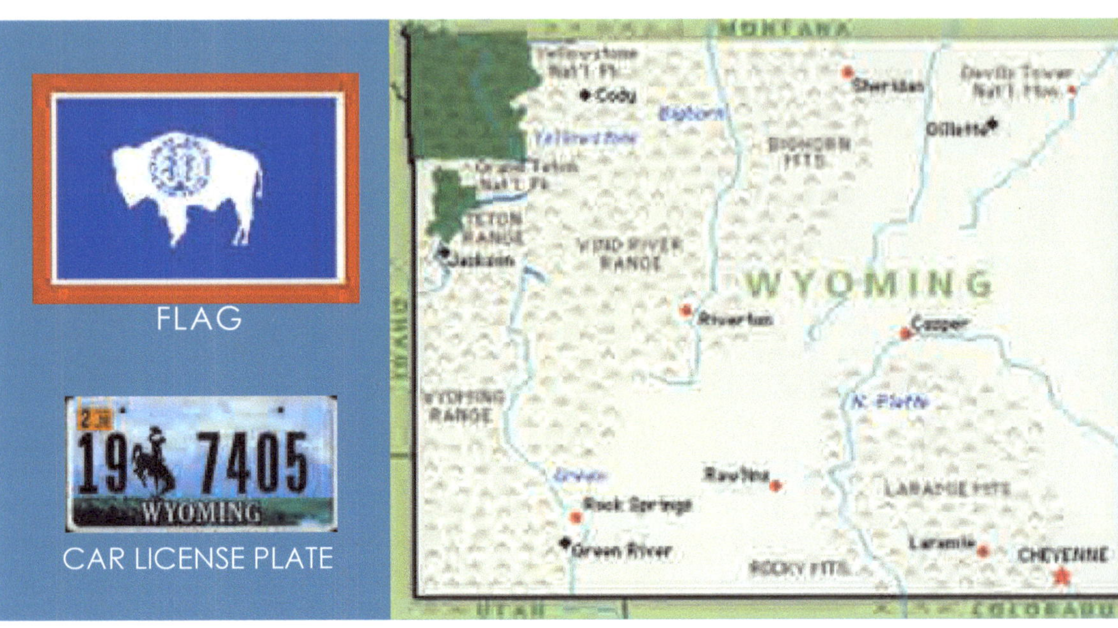

Cottonwood
Salicaceae Populus deltoides

Western Meadow Lark
Sturnella neglecta

Indian Paintbrush
Castilleja linariaefolia

FAMOUS WYOMINGITES

James Bridger	Trapper, guide and storyteller
John Colter	Trader
June Etta Downey	Educator
Thomas Fitzpatrick	Mountain man and guide
Curt Gowdy	Sportscaster
Tom Horn	Detective
Isabel Jewell	Actress
Velma Linford	Writer
Ted Olson	Writer
John "Portugee" Phillips	Frontiersman
Jackson Pollock	Painter
Alan Swallow	Publisher and author
Francis E. Warren	First state governor
Chief Washakie	Chief of the Shoshone
James G. Watt	Former secretary of the Interior

CAPITAL CITY	CHEYENNE
POPULATION	493,782 50TH LARGEST STATE
ENTERED STATEHOOD	JULY 10, 1890, 44TH STATE
BORDER STATE	COLORADO, IDAHO, MONTANA, NEBRASKA, SOUTH DAKOTA, UTAH
HIGHEST POINT	GANNETT PEAK, 13,804 FT.
LOWEST POINT	BELLE FOURCHE RIVER, 3,099 FT
TOPOGRAPHY	
AREA	97,105 SQUARE MILES – 10TH LAND SIZE 714 SQUARE MILES – 9TH WATER SIZE
ECONOMY	
AGRICULTURE	CATTLE, SUGAR BEETS, SHEEP, HAY WHEAT
INDUSTRY	MINING, CHEMICAL PRODUCTS, LUMBER AND WOOD PRODUCTS, PRINTING AND PUBLISHING, MACHINERY, TOURISM

- Wyoming was the first state to give women the right to vote.
- Wyoming has the lowest population of all 50 United States.
- The Red Desert in south central Wyoming drains neither to the east nor to the west. The continental divide splits and goes around the desert on all sides leaving the basin without normal drainage.
- The Wind River actually changes its name in the middle of the stream becoming the Big Horn River at a site at the north end of the Wind River Canyon, where each year the Native Americans hold a ceremony de-picting the "Wedding of the Waters."

R E F E R E N

The following web sites were used to gather information on each state:
15Q.NET, 50STATES.COM, NETSTATE.COM, WIKIPEDIA.ORG, WEATHER.GOV

All of the information included in "Here In America" is from the 'net except for certain photographs. Thanks go to the following sources per state.

CE PAGE

REFERENCE PAGE

ALABAMA Bird - George Earle Shankle, PhD. Tree by Aviahuisman Photography on Dreamstime.com
Information: Clyde Sherman, meddy42, Jhirsch39, Gabbatha, Ken Tarter, Ifreda.
Cotton Harvesting Photo: Kittie Woolliscroft
Cotton Field Photo: Kittie Woolliscroft
Real Estate near Dothan Al Photo: Kittie Woolliscroft

ALASKA Bird – Courtesy National Park Service, Tree - ASK.COM, Information: Clyde Sherman, meddy42, Jhirsch39, Gabbatha, Ken Tarter, Ifreda.
All Photos: Veronica Taylor

ARIZONA Tree by Eutoch on Dreamstime.Com. Information: Clyde Sherman, meddy42, Jhirsch39, Gabbatha, Ken Tarter, Ifreda
Grand Canyon with Karen Photo by Keith Rhode
Real Estate Photo by Butterfunk.com

ARKANSAS Tree by Nmorozova on Dreamstime.com, Information: Clyde Sherman, meddy42, Jhirsch39, Gabbatha, Ken Tarter, Ifreda.
Hot Springs Hotel Photo; Kittie Woolliscroft
Scenic view of the Ozark Mountains off Highway 123 by Arkansas Tourism Official Site

CALIFORNIA Tree by Ed Cooper, Redwood Empire. Information: Clyde Sherman, meddy42, Jhirsch39, Gabbatha,
Ken Tarter, Ifreda
Death Valley National Park Route 374, Death Valley, California, USA by Creative Commons
-
Golden Gate Bridge Photo by Aaron Knight on Dreamstime.com

COLORADO Tree by Inger Anne Hulbaekdal on Dremstime.com. Thanks to Travel & Tourism Authority General Information: Clyde Sherman, meddy42, Jhirsch39, Gabbatha, Ken Tarter, Ifreda,
Rocky Mountain area Photos Ava Betz

CONNECTICUT Tree by Janis Svitins on Dreamstime.com Information: Clyde Sherman, meddy42, Jhirsch39, Gabbatha, Ken Tarter, Ifreda, INTERESTING ITEMS Sandy Kreutter.
PHOTOS: "Used by permission of the State of Connecticut".
Mansfield Hollow State Park Kim Aberle
Bushnell Park
Hartford Skyline from State Capitol Thomas Rotkiewicz

DELAWARE

Tree by Connie Larsen on Dreamstime.com Thanks to GREATER WILINGTON CONVENTION & VISTORS BUREAU and the DELWARE ECONOMIC DEVELOPMENT OFFICE, Information: Clyde Sherman, meddy42, Jhirsch39, Gabbatha, Ken Tarter, Ifreda,
Delaware photo from the Internet, State of Delaware. No other reference.

FLORIDA

Tree by Adinalee on Dreamstime.Com Information: Clyde Sherman, meddy42, Jhirsch39, Gabbatha, Ken Tarter, Ifreda,
White sandy beach in Panama City Photo Kittie Woolliscroft
Sunshine Skyway from Apollo Beach Photo Kittie Woolliscroft
Sand Cranes in Orlando Photo Kittie Woolliscroft

GEORGIA

Tree by Stacey Lynn Payne on Dreamstime.com Information: Clyde Sherman, meddy42, Jhirsch39, Gabbatha, Ken Tarter, Ifreda,
LaGrange off 219 Photo Kittie Woolliscroft
West Point Lake near LaGrange Photo Kittie Woolliscroft

HAWAII

Photo of State Tree not available Information: Clyde Sherman, meddy42, Jhirsch39, Gabbatha, Ken Tarter, Ifreda
Oahu Mountains .
Palm Trees PacHD.com.
Road Butterfunk.com

IDAHO

Tree by Melinda Naqy on Dreamstime.com Information: Clyde Sherman, meddy42, Jhirsch39, Gabbatha, Ken Tarter, Ifreda
Mormon Temple Photo L. Nikki Betz-Quick
Mountain range Photo L. Nikki Betz-Quick

ILLINOIS

Tree by Janis Svitins on Dreamstime.com Information: Clyde Sherman, meddy42, Jhirsch39, Gabbatha, Ken Tarter, Ifreda.
Photo of Spoon River Scenic Drive, Fulton County from Butterfunk.com

INDIANA

Tree by Hurry on Dreamstime.com Information: Jack Daniels, Mandy Paige, Beth Markley, Clyde Sherman, meddy42, Jhirsch39, Gabbatha, Ken Tarter, Ifreda/
Photo of Quilt Gardens in Amish Country from visitindiana.com
Photo of Covered Bridge Capital of the World from visitindiana.com

IOWA

Tree- Netstate.com, Information: Clyde Sherman, meddy42, Jhirsch39, Gabbatha, Ken Tarter, Ifreda
A snowy day in Iowa from BUTTERFUNK.COM
A waterfall by the roadside from BUTTERFUNK.COM

KANSAS

Tree by Terrance Emerson on Dreamstime.com Thanks to Kansas Wheathearts, Jeff Newman, Peter J. Freund, rbraig Information: Clyde Sherman, meddy42, Jhirsch39, Gabbatha, Ken Tarter, Ifreda.
Harvesting at Sunset Photo Ava Betz

Kansas Country Photo Ava Betz

KENTUCKY Tree by Hurry on Dreamstime.com Thanks to Kentucky Department of Travel, John D. Dowd, Mandy Paige, DeLores Wiggins, Wayne Shelton, David Grossman, Cleamon Inman,

Jody

Odonnell,. Information: Clyde Sherman, meddy42, Jhirsch39, Gabbatha, Ken Tarter,

Ifreda.

Autumn in Kentucky from Butterfunk.com
Real Estate in Kentucky from Butterfunk.com

LOUISIANNA Tree by Jennifer Thompson on Dreamstime.com Information: Sandy Kreutter,
Karolyn

Goss. Clyde Sherman, meddy42, Jhirsch39, Gabbatha, Ken Tarter, Ifreda.
New Orleans across the river Photo Kittie Woolliscroft
Steamboat ride Photo Kittie Woolliscroft
Typical home Photo Kittie Woolliscroft

MAINE. Tree by Mariusz Jurgielewicz on Dreamstime.com Information: David C. Weiler, Henry Miller, Cindy Coffin, Larryel, Cheryl Emerson. Clyde Sherman, meddy42, Jhirsch39,

Gabbatha,

Ken Tarter, Ifreda.
Lighthouse Photo Angela Wilkenson
Real Estate Photo Angela Wilkenson

MARYLAND Tree by Janis Svitins on Dreamstime.com Information: Beverly Miller, Steve Turner, Istr8nm, Ifreda. Clyde Sherman, meddy42, Jhirsch39, Gabbatha, Ken Tarter, Ifreda.
Maryland Heights from Butterfunk.com
Loys Covered Bridge from Butterfunk.com

MASSACHUSSETS Tree by Maksym Bondarchuck on Dreamstime.com Information: Sandy Kreutter, David C. Weiler, Peg, Ethel Duggans, Mary Ferrara, Wakelings, MATD27. Clyde Sherman, meddy42, Jhirsch39, Gabbatha, Ken Tarter, Ifreda.
Shelburne Falls from Butterfunk.com
BOSTON from Butterfunk.com

MICHIGAN Tree by Mariusz Jurgielewicz on Dreamstime.com Information: Ruby Simmons, Eric Merriam, James Toscas, Jan Lee Asmann, Janet Kijek, James H. Jackson, Katrina & Bryan Tollenaar , Clyde Sherman, meddy42, Jhirsch39, Gabbatha, Ken Tarter, Ifreda.
Autumn in the UP from Butterfunk.com
Michigan Waterfall from Butterfunk.com

MINNESOTA Tree by Jakub Ceipek on Dreamstime.com Information: Phil Douglas, Ward Blumer, Clyde Sherman, meddy42, Jhirsch39, Gabbatha, Ken Tarter, Ifreda.
Steam Boat Bay Gull Lake Minnesota Butterfunk.com
Snowy trees Butterfunk.com

MISSISSIPPI Tree by Puma330 on Dreamstime.com Source: "Mississippi", published by the office of
the

Secretary of State Information: Ron Collins, Greg Maxedon,Clyde Sherman, meddy42,

Jhirsch39, Gabbatha, Ken Tarter, lfreda.
Plantation House Photo by author Kenneth R. Taylor

MISSOURI Tree by Michael Smith on Dreamstime.com Information: Charles Andrew Humfeld, Gene Kerr, PMary25491, Scott Peterson, Seatac57, Clyde Sherman, meddy42, Jhirsch39,

Gabbatha,

Ken Tarter, lfreda.
St Louis Arial photo Butterfunk.com
Missouri River photo Butterfunk.com

MONTANA Tree by Pancaketom on Dreamstime Information: 7mbuell, Joel & Katrina, Travel Montana,. Clyde Sherman, meddy42, Jhirsch39, Gabbatha, Ken Tarter, lfreda.
Home on the Range Photo Jack Ancell
View from Snow bowl Photo Butterfunk.com

NEBRASKA Tree by Terrance Emerson on Dreamstime.com Information: Nancy Schreiner, Diane Robinson, Mike Kuhn, Scott Peterson, Stephanie Hamilton, rbrummers5, Clyde Sherman, meddy42, Jhirsch39, Gabbatha, Ken Tarter, lfreda.
Both Nebraska Real Estate photos from Butterfunk.com

NEVADA Tree by Andrea Hornackova on Dreamstime.com Nevada Film Office - Updates and corrections courtesy of Guy Louis Rocha, Nevada State Archivist , Information: Clyde Sherman, meddy42, Jhirsch39, Gabbatha, Ken Tarter, lfreda.
Looking down from Hoover Dam Photo Kittie Woolliscroft

NEW HAMPSHIRE Tree by John Anderson on Dreamstime.com Information: Clyde Sherman, meddy42, Jhirsch39, Gabbatha, Ken Tarter, lfreda.
Beeches Birches and Firs Photo Butterfunk.com
New Hampshire Photo Butterfunk.com

NEW JERSEY Tree by Fedotishe on Dreamstime.com
Information: JAMESON530, Timothy Phillips, William A. Evans, Clyde Sherman, meddy42, Jhirsch39, Gabbatha, Ken Tarter, lfreda.
Independence Hall Photo Butterfunk.com
A Fire Rainbow over New Jersey Photo Butterfunk.com

NEW MEXICO Bird by John James Audubon, F. R. SS. L. & E. Information: JP Dur, Crucesdale, Gary Harper, Derek Benjamin, Tom Bombaci, Jr., Darla Boyd, Beth Markley Clyde Sherman, meddy42, Jhirsch39, Gabbatha, Ken Tarter, lfreda.
Acoma Photo from Butterfunk.com
Rock City Photo from Butterfunk.com

NEW YORK Tree by Melinda Fawver on Dreamstime.com Thanks to: New York State Division of Tourism, John D. Dowd, Maggie Sebastian, and BJKintigh Information: Clyde Sherman, meddy42, Jhirsch39, Gabbatha, Ken Tarter, lfreda.
City Photos Veronica Taylor

NORTH CAROLINA Tree by Aviahuisman Photography on Dremstime.com Information: Rhonda G. Moore, Doreen Rearick, Dione Willis, Waf518205, Jeff Rickert, Stuart Laue, Jresce, Paula Toppings, RHEMC, Clyde Sherman, meddy42, Jhirsch39, Gabbatha, Ken Tarter, lfreda.

Biltmore Estate in Ashville Photo Veronica Taylor

NORTH DAKOTA

Tree by Maksym Bondarchuck on Dreamstime.com. Information: Galbraith, Us4UpNorth,. Clyde Sherman, meddy42, Jhirsch39, Gabbatha, Ken Tarter, lfreda.
Sunflower field Butterfunk.com
Badlands Butterfunk.com

OHIO

Tree by Maksym Bondarchuck on Dreamstime.com Information: Greg Maxedon, Kathy Liess, Robert Whitworth, J Williams, Laura Campbell, SanTan Man, Pat Holz, Clyde Sherman, meddy42, Jhirsch39, Gabbatha, Ken Tarter, lfreda.
Fallen Heroes Memorial Butterfunk.com
Bellaire Butterfunk.com

OKLAHOMA

Tree from Zhigong Zhang on Dreamstime.com Informational: Donnie, Bryan Nies, TobeCT, Rachel Burnsed, trophies, Wallysden Clyde Sherman, meddy42, Jhirsch39, Gabbatha, Ken Tarter, lfreda.
Spillway creek Butterfunk.com
Oklahoma City Butterfunk.com

OREGON

Tree by Matauw on Dreamstime.com Thanks to: Out West Newspaper, Convention & Visitors Association of Lane County Oregon, Roy Daw, Lana Rose, Ken Lambert, Peter LaPorte, Reid Sanford, David Blanchard . Information Clyde Sherman, meddy42, Jhirsch39, Gabbatha, Ken Tarter, lfreda.
Riverwalk Photo Butterfunk.com
Shasta Lake Photo Butterfunk.com

PENNSYLVANIA

Tree by Dorin S on istockphoto.com Bird by John James Audubon, F. R. SS. L. & E., . Information: MirComer, Madonam, Chrystal, Heather Robertson, Johnny Wang, Landau-Smith, Barb Burba, Jskraptor, Rebecca Kane, John Snyder, Lynn, Clyde Sherman, meddy42, Jhirsch39, Gabbatha, Ken Tarter, lfreda. Bird by John James Audubon, F. R. SS. L. & E., .
Farm from the air Photo Butterfunk.com
Row homes Photo Butterfunk.oom

RHODE ISLAND

Tree by Nikolais Strigins on Dreamstime.com Thanks to: David C. Weiler, Luc Beaufort, Jaisley30, Mjc02865. . Information: Clyde Sherman, meddy42, Jhirsch39, Gabbatha, Ken Tarter, lfreda.
Beach Narragansett Photo Butterfunk.com
Sailing Photo Butterfunk.com

SOUTH CAROLINA

Tree by Adinalee on Dreamstime.com Thanks to: Joyce Myers, Beverly Miller, Diana La Rocque, gaitrie, Randy Cox Information: Clyde Sherman, meddy42, Jhirsch39, Gabbatha, Ken Tarter, lfreda.
Church Photo Butterfunk.com Palm Tree
Photo Butterfunk.com

SOUTH DAKOTA
kkostel,

Tree by Vladimir Daragan on Dreamstime.com Information: Crucesdale, JRB049,

. Clyde Sherman, meddy42, Jhirsch39, Gabbatha, Ken Tarter, lfreda.
Train across the Plain Photo Keith Rhode
Mount Rushmore Photo Kittie Woolliscroft

TENNESSEE

Tree by Hurry on Dreamstime.com Information: Webfacts, Cindy, Gabbatha, Gordon Waters,

Johnny Wang, Clyde Sherman, meddy42, Jhirsch39, Gabbatha, Ken Tarter, Ifreda.
Under the Bridge in Chattanooga Photo Kittie Woolliscroft
A nice place to stay Photo Kittie Woolliscroft

TEXAS

Tree by Yosef Erpert on Dreamstime.com. Information: Clyde Sherman, meddy42, Jhirsch39, Gabbatha, Ken Tarter, Ifreda.
Palo Duro Photo Butterfunk.com
Austin Photo Butterfunk.com

UTAH

Tree by Inger Ane Hulbaekdal on Dreamstime.com Information: Janice Bryant, Utah Facts Online 1997-98, Rebecca, Emma, Clyde Sherman, meddy42, Jhirsch39, Gabbatha, Ken Tarter, Ifreda.
Real Estate – Red Rock Photo Microsoft
Real Estate – Drab Rock Photo Butterfunk.com

VERMONT

Tree by Melinda Fawver on Dreamstime.com Information: David C. Weiler, Clyde Sherman, meddy42, Jhirsch39, Gabbatha, Ken Tarter, Ifreda.
Covered Bridge Photo from Butterfunk.com
Vermont Lake Photo from Butterfunk.com

VIRGINIA

Tree by Karin Hildebrand Lau on Dreamstime.com Informational: Kay Koehler, Darla Boyd, Beth Markley, . Clyde Sherman, meddy42, Jhirsch39, Gabbatha, Ken Tarter, Ifreda.
Ski Lift Photo Butterfunk.com
Uncovered Bridge Photo Butterfunk.com

WASHINGTON

Tree by Tonda on istockphoto.com Bird: By John James Audubon, F. R. SS. L. & E Information: Gerald Moon, Cindy, Daniel Berman, MHus915910, Paul Dexter, Megan Moench, Phillip Buff , . Clyde Sherman, meddy42, Jhirsch39, Gabbatha, Ken Tarter, Ifreda.
Space Needle Photo PHOTOBUCKET.COM
SEATTLE Photo Butterfunk.com

WEST VIRGINIA

Tree by Melinda Fawver on Dreamstime.com Information: Darleen Jeske, Reid M. Webster, Patrick J. McGrath, Sharon Mathis, Michele Wilson, Amma26, Cindy Szajna, Guy Baucher, Valerie McAuliffe . Timothy R Lovell, WV Division of Tourism Clyde Sherman, meddy42, Jhirsch39, Gabbatha, Ken Tarter, Ifreda.
Generating electricity Photo Kittie Woolliscroft
Real Estate near Dry Fork Photo Jack Ancell

WISCONSIN

Tree by Melinda Fawver on Dreamstime.com Bird by JOHN JAMES Audubon, F. R. SS. L. & E Informational: Clyde Sherman, meddy42, Jhirsch39, Gabbatha, Ken Tarter, Ifreda,
St. Croix River boat landing Photo Kittie Woolliscroft
Lake Pepin at sunset Photo Kittie Woolliscroft.

WYOMING

Tree by Terrance Emerson on Dreamstime.com Informational: Clyde Sherman, meddy42, Jhirsch39, Gabbatha, Ken Tarter, Ifreda.
Deer crossing the creek Photo by Kittie Woolliscroft
Buffalo getting a drink Photo by Kittie Woolliscroft

www.ingramcontent.com/pod-product-compliance
Lightning Source LLC
Chambersburg PA
CBHW041925180726
48295CB00003B/79
9781948801034